JUNK
—RECORD OF THE LAST HERO—
KIA ASAMIYA PRESENTS
1

Author / Kia Asamiya
Translator / Yoshihiro Watanabe
Production Artist / Nhung Tran
Cover Artist / Bryce Gunkel
English Adaptation / Ailen Lujo
Editor / Matthew Scrivner
Supervising Editor / Ailen Lujo
V.P. of Operations / Yuki Chung
President / Jennifer Chen

Publisher
DrMaster Publications Inc.
4044 Clipper Ct.
Fremont, CA 94538
www.DrMasterbooks.com

Second Edition: September 2007

ISBN 13: 978-1-59796-107-3
ISBN 10: 1-59796-107-8

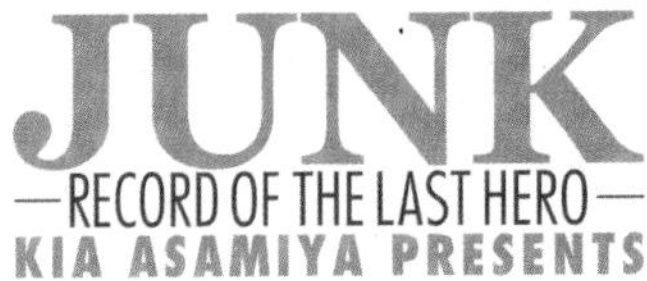

TABLE OF CONTENTS

BOOM
HOW... DID YOU USE YOUR POWER?
WITH THAT POWER...
WHAT DID YOU CHOOSE...
HWOOO

... TO BECOME?
I... DID...?
A GOD...?
A DEVIL...?

JUSTICE. 1:......JUNK BOY
WHO KNOWS...?

JUNK
RECORD OF THE LAST HERO
KIA ASAMIYA

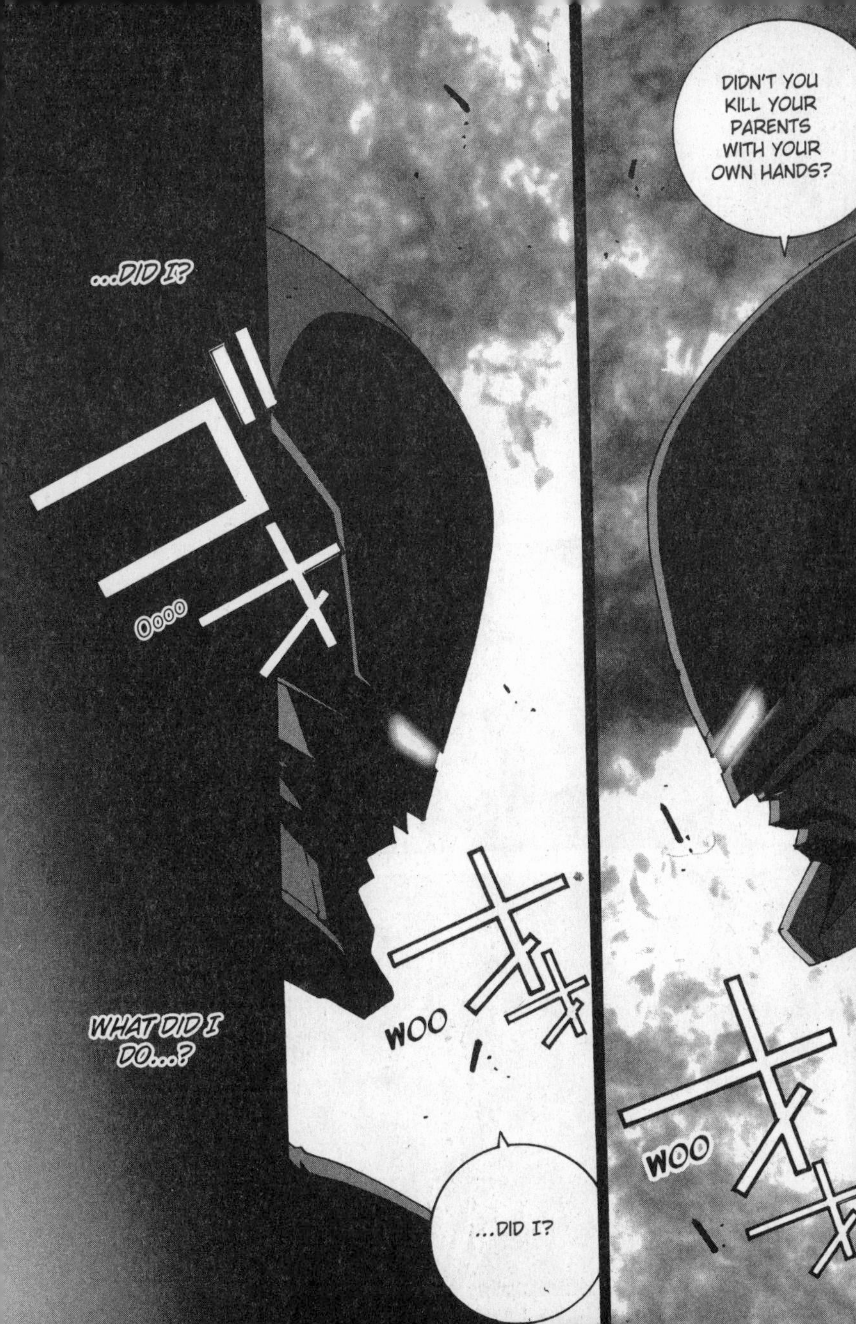

DIDN'T YOU KILL YOUR PARENTS WITH YOUR OWN HANDS?
WOO
...DID I?
WOO
...DID I?
Oooo
WHAT DID I DO...?

ARE YOU AWAKE, HIRO-CHAN?

I'LL LEAVE YOUR BREAKFAST HERE,

ガバ
Whosh
UH...

ガタ
SKREEK

ガチャ
rattle

バタン
Slam

WHEN IS HIRO PLANNING ON STARTING BACK AT SCHOOL?
I'M NOT SURE...
YOU SHOULD TALK TO HIM, TOO...

I'VE ALREADY TOLD HIM EVERYTHING I COULD.
HE RESPONDS VIOLENTLY, SO I CAN'T SAY ANYTHING MORE.

A JUNIOR HIGH-SCHOOL STUDENT HAS COMMITTED A TOTAL OF SEVEN ASSAULT CASES AND...
...

IN ALL OF THESE CASES, FEMALE STUDENTS HAVE BEEN ASSAULTED FROM BEHIND WITH A HAMMER.
WHAT IF HIRO WERE TO COMMIT SUCH A CRIME...?
TO DO SO, HE'D ACTUALLY NEED TO COME OUT OF HIS ROOM...
I'M OFF...
Y... YES

HAVE A GOOD DAY.
GOOD MORNING.

GOOD MORNING, AUNTIE
GOOD MORNING.
RYOKO-CHAN, SORRY FOR ALL THE TROUBLE.
Thump
Thump
IT'S ALL RIGHT.

I CAN'T JUST LEAVE HIM ALONE. BESIDES, HE'S MY CLASSMATE.
CLICK
CLICK
...

I'LL LEAVE A COPY OF YESTERDAY'S CLASS NOTES HERE.
...
ARE YOU LISTENING TO ME, HIRO-KUN?

CLIK
CLIK
CLIK
CLIK
CLIK
CLIK
CLIK
CLIK
CLIK

CLIK
CLIK
CLIK

WELCOME TO THE
JUNK
GO!!

HM?

!
CLIK

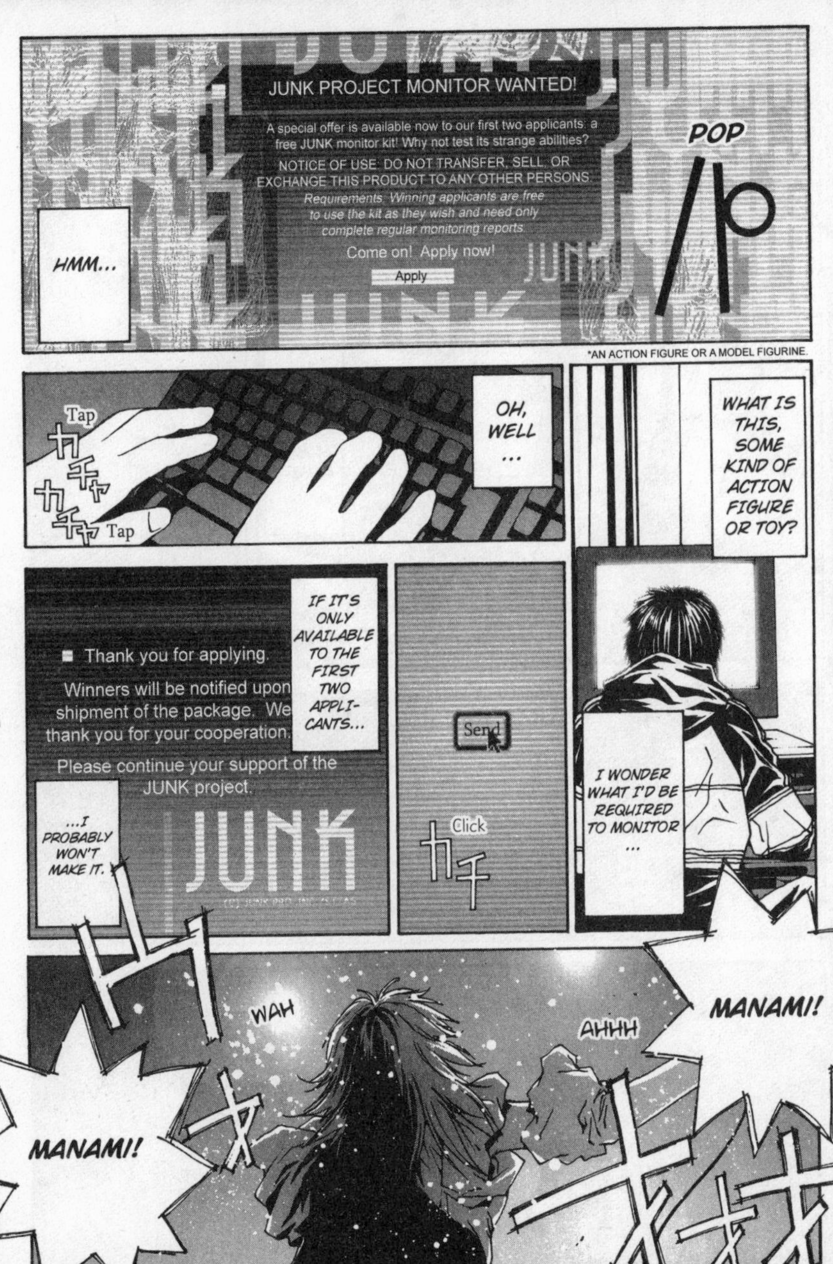

*AN ACTION FIGURE OR A MODEL FIGURINE.

IT'S MANAMI.
MANAMI.

SHE'S CUTE...
BUT SHE LIVES IN A DIFFERENT WORLD THAN I DO.

EVEN THOUGH WE'RE BOTH HUMAN BEINGS ...
BUT IT CAN'T BE HELPED.

Wooooh

MMM...
NO!

OK, PULL HIS PANTS DOWN. THE UNDERWEAR, TOO.
HA HA HA HA HA HA HA
STOP IT! WHAT ARE YOU GUYS DOING?!

SHUT UP! I DON'T LIKE THE WAY YOUR EYES LOOK.
HEY! HURRY UP WITH THOSE WORMS!

HERE.
STOP IT!

HEY, HOLD HIM STEADY.
I'LL FEED YOU RIGHT NOW, HIRO-KUN.

AUGH!

FWSH
HAH
HAH
HAH
SHIT!
SHIT! DAMN THEM! BASTARDS!!!

DAMN THEM!

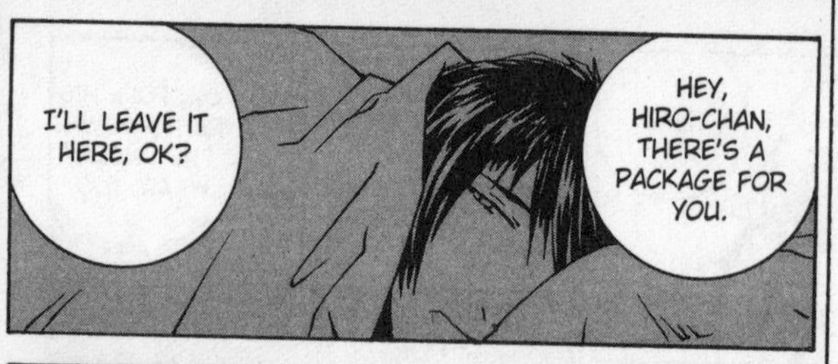
HEY, HIRO-CHAN, THERE'S A PACKAGE FOR YOU.
I'LL LEAVE IT HERE, OK?

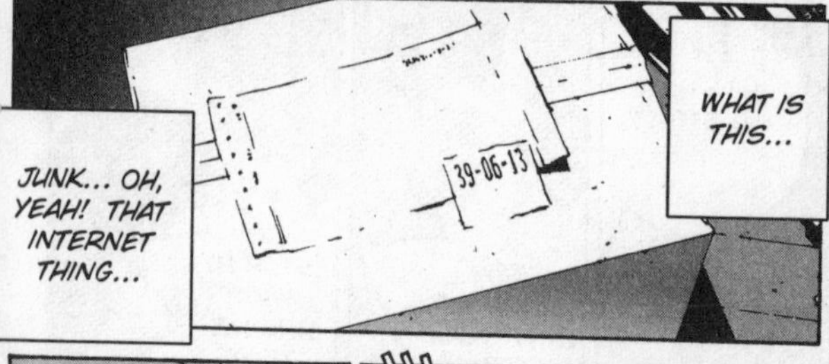
WHAT IS THIS...
39-06-13
JUNK... OH, YEAH! THAT INTERNET THING...

IT ARRIVED ALREADY! AND I'M ONE OUT OF THE TWO?
AMAZ-ING.
RIP
RIP

WHAT THE HELL IS THIS?

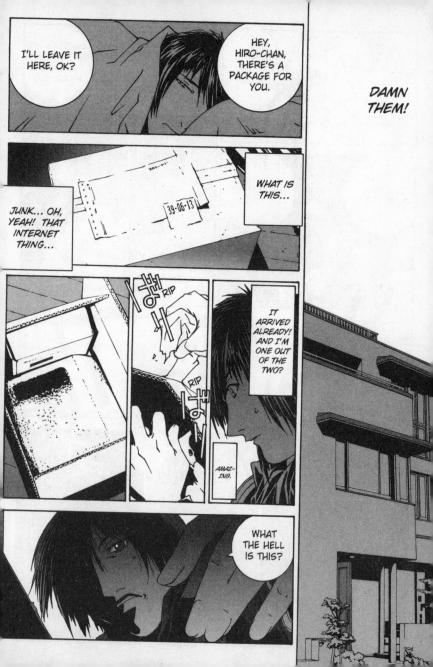

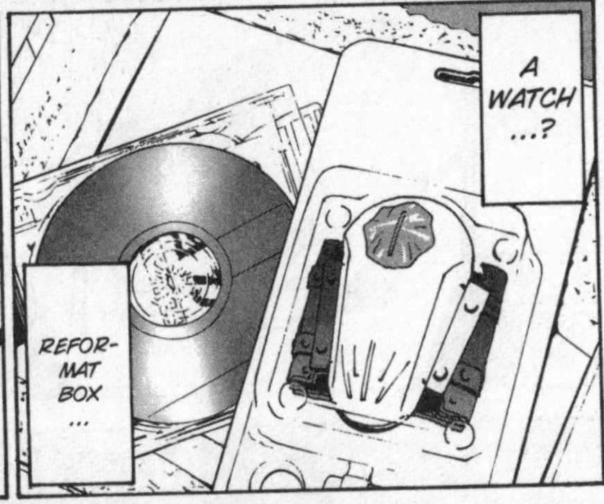

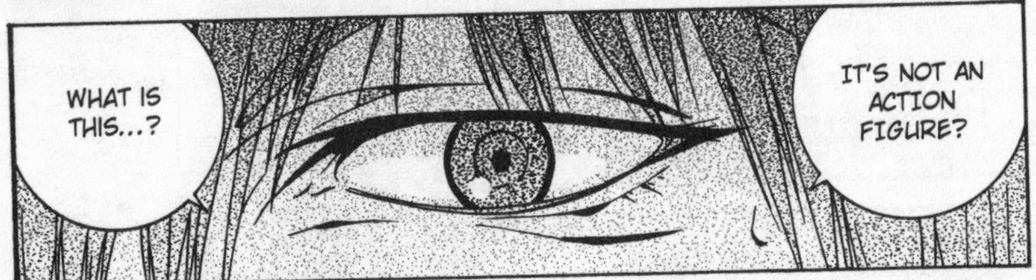

SIGH... MAN, WHAT IS THIS?

I DON'T NEED A WATCH...

I'LL SELL IT ON EBAY.

CLICK

カッ

FUJIFILM

CLICK

... BUT IT'S A WEIRD WATCH.

MENU / ON

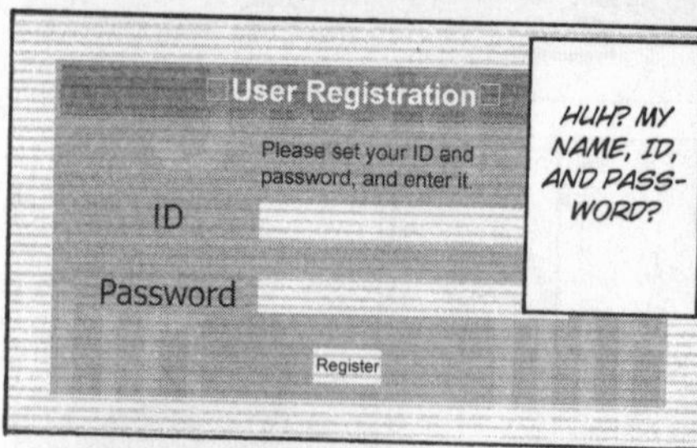

STAB

UNTIL THE RED LED LIGHT TURNS ON...

PUT MY FINGER INTO THIS?

DNA Register

DNA REGIS-TER?

Connect the USB cable for the DNA registering unit that is included in the package.

Please follow these instructions carefully. Insert your finger into the selector portion and press firmly untilfirmly until the red LED light turns on.

After DNA samply, please answer all questions to the best of your ability on the Data screen. Main bracelet use aire requires DNA registration. Please connect USB cable to slot under bracelet and press button until confirmation is indicated. When light blinks, registration is complete is complete.

OW!

W-W-W-WHAT IS THIS?

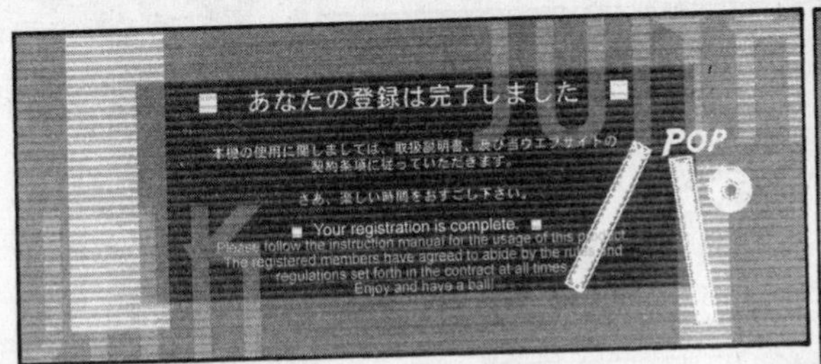
あなたの登録は完了しました
Your registration is complete.
Please follow the instruction manual for the usage of this
The registered members have agreed to abide by the
regulations set forth in the contract at all times.
Enjoy and have a ball!
POP

UNLUCKY
...

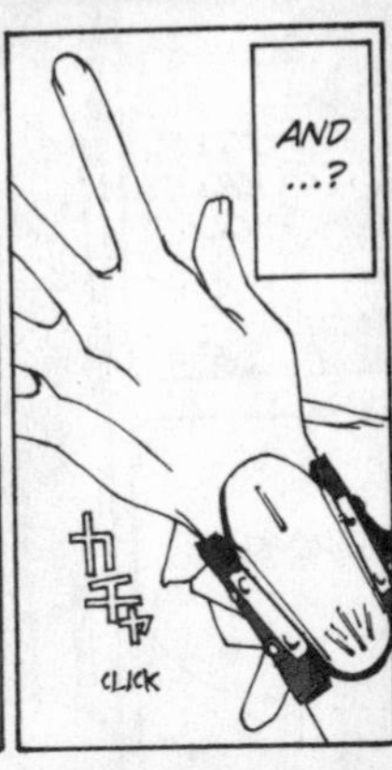
AND
...?
カチャ
CLICK

HMM?
MMM?
WHAT?
LIKE THIS?

AND THIS?
PI
ピッ

HUH?

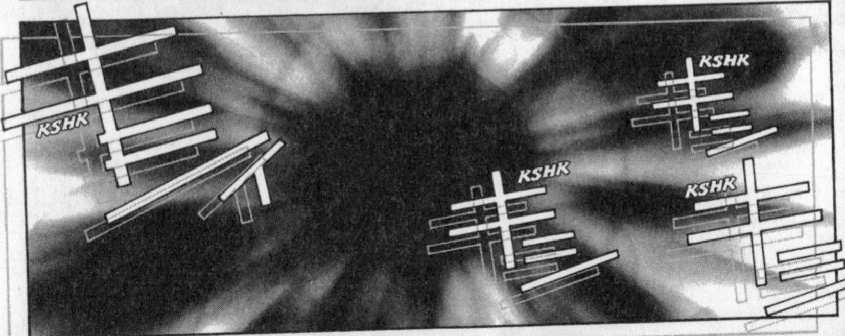
KSHK
KSHK
KSHK
KSHK

OH... WHA ?
HIRO-CHAN? WHAT'S GOING ON?
IS SOME-THING WRONG?
N... NOTHING'S WRONG! YOU'D BETTER NOT COME UP HERE!
I'LL KILL YOU!
A... ALL RIGHT.
HIRO-CHAN...
Pin Pon!
WHO IS IT?
NICE TO MEET YOU, MADAM.
I'M TSUJIDO, A COUNSELOR SENT BY THE YOUTH EDUCATIONAL BOARD.

AH... YES, THE COUNSELOR WE REQUESTED. PLEASE COME IN.
IT'S OK, MADAM. I JUST STOPPED BY SINCE I WAS IN THE NEIGHBORHOOD. WE'RE NOT SUPPOSED TO BEGIN HIS COUNSELING...

I'M HERE TODAY TO SAY HELLO ...
UNTIL TOMORROW.

I WANTED TO SEE HIRO-KUN, AS WELL, BUT...
AH... UM... RIGHT NOW ISN'T...

I GUESS IT'S NOT A GOOD TIME.

THEN I'LL COME BACK TOMORROW AT ONE.
Y... YES, WE'LL BE LOOKING FORWARD TO IT.

...

Plunk

SERIOUSLY?!
WHAT IS THIS...?

WOW!
Scrnch
OH!
SMASH

F... FOR REAL...

WHAT'S GOING ON?
Plop

THIS IS...

THIS IS...

IF THINGS CAN CHANGE FROM THIS,

IT'S WORTH THE MONEY.

SO, THE COUNSELOR IS STARTING TOMORROW?

YES, HE CAME BY TODAY TO SAY HELLO...

SQUEAK
カラカラ
SQUEAK

Thap

HAH.
IT'S BEEN HALF A YEAR SINCE I BREATHED THE OUTSIDE AIR.

IT TASTES GREAT ...
VOOSH

HA HA HA
HA HA HA HA
HA! HA HA
HA HA HA HA
HA HA!
OOOO
SLOSH
STAB
THAP

WOOOO
THIS IS GREAT! AMAZING! WHAT A GIFT!
Splat
Splat
Splap
Splap
...
HEH HEH HEH!
IT'S REALLY REAL.

*ONIGIRI IS A JAPANESE RICE BALL.

WAH HA HA HA HA HA HA HA!
WHAT THE HELL ARE YOU?! THAT SOME KINDA COSPLAY?*
*COSPLAY IS SHORT FOR COSTUME PLAY.
YOU...
WHAT ARE Y... YO....
CRASH
...
FLING
NNNGH

CLANK
DAMN YOU!
VOOM
CRASH
HUH? HUH?
...
CLANG

...
Smash
AYG-HHH!
STAY AWAY!

WOOH
WOOH
Fwip
HMMMM ...
HA HA HA HA HA HA!
I'VE BEEN REBORN!
SQUEEAK
HOW MANY MONTHS HAS IT BEEN SINCE I LAST LAUGHED?

HAVE YOU HEARD?
ABOUT THAT CONVENIENCE STORE LAST NIGHT, RIGHT?
ALL THREE OF THE YOUNG VICTIMS WERE CRITICALLY INJURED, AND THE ONLY WITNESSES WERE THE STORE CLERK AND A BUSINESSMAN THAT WAS AT THE SCENE...
IT'S ON, IT'S ON.
LAST NIGHT, AN UNIDENTI-FIED MAN ASSAULTED SOMEONE RIGHT HERE, IN FRONT OF THIS CONVE-NIENCE STORE.
IT'S SO FRIGHTENING.
DURING THE DAY IT'S FINE, BUT AT NIGHT, THAT CONVENIENT STORE BECAME THEIR HANG-OUT SPOT. IT WAS PRETTY BAD.
SO, AREN'T THERE PEOPLE OUT THERE WHO ARE PLEASED TO HEAR THIS?
IT'S SO TERRIBLE... BUT THOSE THREE WERE INFAMOUS THUGS AROUND HERE.
THIS IS GREAT. IT'S ACTUALLY ON TV.
HEH HEH HEH HEH.

IT'S DAD! HA HA!
SO, THE TV CREW IS REALLY THERE!
HEY!
Mysterious man?
Assault near a convenient store.

!!
HIRO-CHAN?

THIS IS GOOD! THIS NEWS ABOUT ME...
I'LL RECORD THEM ALL, ALONG WITH THE TALK SHOWS.

IT'S OK, MA'AM. I'LL TAKE IT FROM HERE.
B... BUT?

EEK!
WHAM
HEY, ARE YOU HIRO-KUN?
!

I'M COUNSELOR TSUJIDO.

NICE TO MEET YA! BY THE WAY, I'VE GOT A QUESTION TO ASK.

ゴォォォォォォ
WOOOO
HMPH.
HMPH.
HMPH.
HMPH.

EVEN THOUGH THERE HAVE BEEN CASES LIKE THIS EVERY NIGHT, I HAVEN'T SEEN ANY IRREFUTABLE EVIDENCE THAT THESE ASSAULTS ARE ACTUALLY HAPPENING.

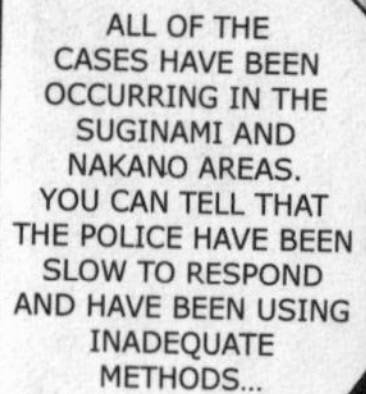

THAT SON OF A BITCH!

IF I GET MY HANDS ON YOU!!

WIIIT

I RECORDED A LOT... I SHOULD BURN IT TO A DVD.

ANOTHER THING...

AS THE CONTRACT INSTRUCTS, I'VE BEEN SENDING IN MY MONITORING DATA TO THE SPECIFIED LOCATION EVERY DAY.

ALL THERE IS TO DO IS TO TAKE OUT THE SD CARD FROM THE WATCH AND INSERT IT INTO THE SLOT. THEN CLICK ON THE PICTURE THAT COMES UP.

BUT... FOR WHAT REASON...

ARE THEY LETTING ME DO THIS?

AND FOR FREE!

THIS POWER IS MINE NOW.

OH, WELL. I SHOULDN'T THINK ABOUT COMPLICATED THINGS.

UM... MAY I COME IN?

HE PROBABLY WON'T LET ME IN AGAIN.

...

GO AHEAD... BUT THE ROOM'S MESSY.

HUH?

O... OK.

HE NEVER LET ME IN HIS ROOM BEFORE...

KCHK

TAKE A SEAT WHEREVER.

SO, WHAT BRINGS YOU HERE TODAY?

CLIK

CLIK

...

I HAVEN'T SEEN YOU IN A WHILE... RYOKO.

AH...

SS

GRP
WHA...
Thum
EEEEK!
STOP IT! I'LL SCREAM!
GO AHEAD. MY MOM WON'T COME.
HEY...
STOP ...
IT...
PLK
SLAP

SLAM
Thum
Thum
Thum
Thum
...
THAP
...
OW...

SKREKKKK

I'M ALONG SUGINAMI KANNANA ST. THERE'S NOTHING HERE!

WHAT WILL YOU DO TONIGHT?

HUH?

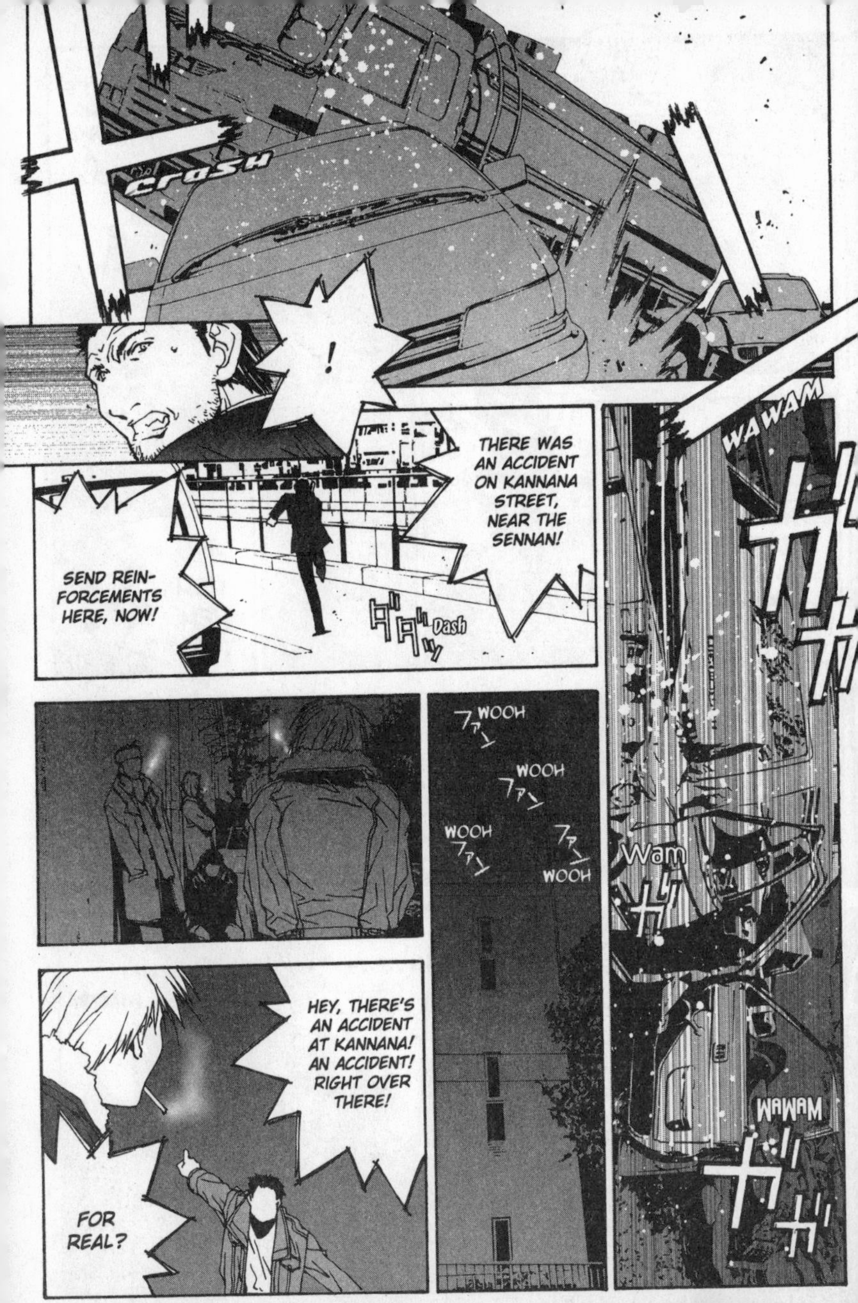
CRASH
!
THERE WAS AN ACCIDENT ON KANNANA STREET, NEAR THE SENNAN!
SEND REIN-FORCEMENTS HERE, NOW!
Dash
WA WAM
WOOH
WOOH
WOOH
WOOH
Wam
HEY, THERE'S AN ACCIDENT AT KANNANA! AN ACCIDENT! RIGHT OVER THERE!
FOR REAL?
WAWAM

WHA-WHAT'S THIS ALL OF A SUDDEN
HEY! THAT'S MY BIKE!
CRASH
VOOSH
LET'S GO TAKE A LOOK!
HEH HEH HEH.

GOOD EVENING.
PUNKS.

THI... THIS GUY...
IS HE THAT GUY? FOR REAL?
IS THIS FOR REAL?
GRRK
YOU CAN PROBABLY SEE THAT FOR YOURSELF.

YES.

AS LONG AS THESE GUYS ...
AS LONG AS THESE GUYS AREN'T AROUND!

HEY, DRIVER, CAN YOU HEAR ME? IS THERE ANY PART THAT YOU CAN'T MOVE?
OO
OO
WOO
WHERE'S THE AMBULANCE?! AND BRING ME THAT CUTTER!

CRAP! HURRY UP AND GET THE DRIVER OUT!
VZZ VZZ

HURRY ...
SHUM
THWAM

!
CRCKLE
CRCKLE
CRCKLE

THAP
Vashoom
HE... HEY! YOU'RE...
KBOOM
AUGH!
AH!
...
Vashom

IF ONLY I HAD THIS POWER SOONER...

HA HA HA.
AUGH!
YOU WON'T ESCAPE!
DAMMIT! DAMMIT!
WHY ARE WE BEING CHASED?!
!
TWO MORE TO GO...

Swack
ONE LEFT!

EEEEEEK!

FOUND HIM!

DASH

Woosh

DAMMIT.

WHOA!

Thud

Thud

Thud

IT'S THAT! THAT! CAMERA, GET A SHOT OF THAT GUY! HURRY!

IT'S THE PATROL CARS. IT'S THE POLICE.

HEY... A CAMERA... SO THE TV CREW IS HERE... I'LL BE ON TOMORROW'S TABLOID TV SHOWS AGAIN.

TIME UP
It is the deadline. It is neces
cancel and carry out cool
of the set early.
There is a risk of the
releasing automat
It is dangerous
OOPS ...
SMASH
Shimmer...
ユラ...
GULP.
Kshhhh
カハー

ガシャ
CHA-CHINK
ガシャ
CHA-CHINK

CHA-CHINK
ガシャ
CHA-CHINK
ガシャ

GET BACK, IT'S DANGEROUS.
Y... YES.

DON'T MOVE!

HURRY UP WITH THE CAMERA! WHAT ARE YOU DOING?!
DON'T PUSH! JEEZ! IT'S LIKE NEW YORK!

VZZM
THE TV CREW NEEDS TO GET BACK!
...

Vashom

PA PA
PA PA
PA
PA PA
PA
DIRECTION OF HIRO-KUN'S HOUSE ...?!
DASH
THAT DIRECTION IS...
DON'T SHOOT!
GO AFTER THAT THING!
THUMP
THUMP
THUMP
THUMP
THAT DEVIL...
IS GOING TO HIRO-KUN'S HOUSE?

HIRO-KUN!
HEY, EVERY-ONE! RUN!
KBLAM
Dom
Dom
HURRY! RUN!
CHA-CHING
IT WENT INSIDE THAT HOUSE!
SURROUND IT! SURROUND IT! NOW!
KABOOM

BOOOOM
WHA...
CRACKLE CRACKLE CRACKLE
CRACKLE CRACKLE CRACKLE

ゴォォォ

VWOOOSH

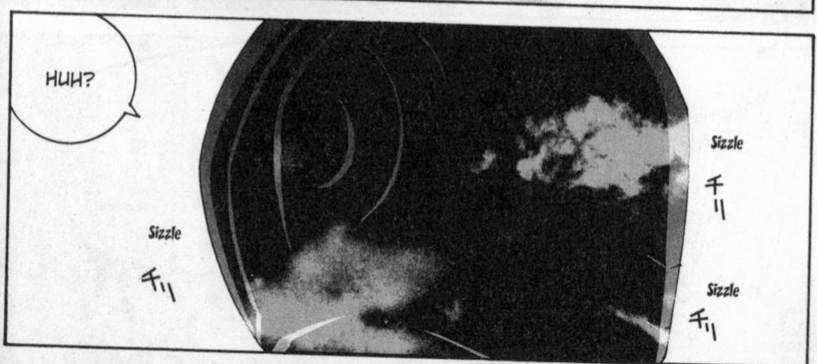

JUSTICE 2: JUNK LIFE

I HAVE STUDIED YOU.
WASN'T THIS YOUR HOME? YOU'VE JUST KILLED YOUR PARENTS WITH YOUR OWN HANDS.
I DID?
DID I?
WOOOOOSH
ANYWAY, WE HAVE TO GET OUT OF HERE.
I... I DID...
CRACKLE
CRACKLE
CRACKLE
CRCK
VZZT
!

AH...
Fft
Grsp
...
FZZLE
GWOOOOOOH
FZZLE
FZZLE
CRACKLE
CRACKLE
VASHOOM
CRCK
WOOH
WOOH
WOOH

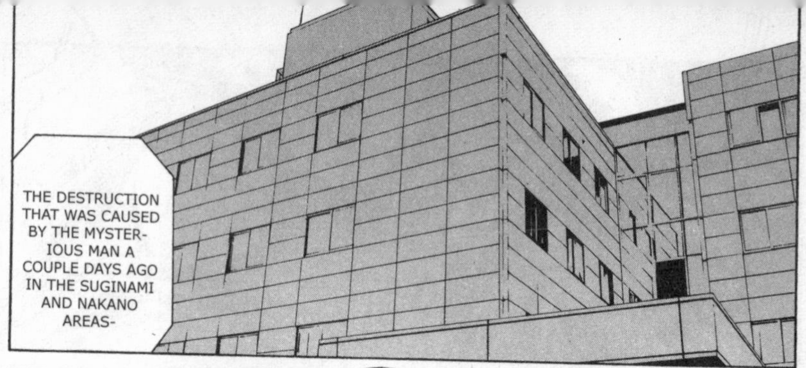
THE DESTRUCTION THAT WAS CAUSED BY THE MYSTERIOUS MAN A COUPLE DAYS AGO IN THE SUGINAMI AND NAKANO AREAS-

HAS CEASED ALL OF A SUDDEN, EVER SINCE A FIRE IN THE SOUTH OF SUGINAMI AREA.
...
THOUGH THERE HAVE BEEN REPORTS OF A SIMILAR MYSTERIOUS FIGURE IN AKASAKA AND ROPPONGI-

DID I... LOSE EVERYTHING...
ALL THAT IS LEFT TO ME IS... JUST MEMORIES.

HIRO-SAN? THERE'S A PACKAGE FOR YOU. ISN'T THAT A SURPRISE?
A PACKAGE?
YES, I'LL JUST LEAVE IT HERE.
ガラス
ビン
セトモノ
ガラス
ビン
セトモノ

...
...
!!
HMPH.
HE HE HE
HE HE.
HMPH
HMPH
HMPH
HMPH
HMPH.
東京都 中野区
新中野 6-80-4
新中野中央病院
結城 比呂
MR. HIRO YUUKI
PLACE TOKYO CITY, CHIYODA AREA,
CENTER, 5-8-320
JUNK SYSTEMS INC.
時計。CD-ROM
WHAT WILL I
CHOOSE TO
BECOME WITH
THIS POWER?
A GOD...
A DEVIL...

RYOKO ONLY HAD A LITTLE BURN ON HER HAND AND SOME MINOR INJURIES, SO SHE'S GOING TO BE DISCHARGED FROM THE HOSPITAL TODAY.
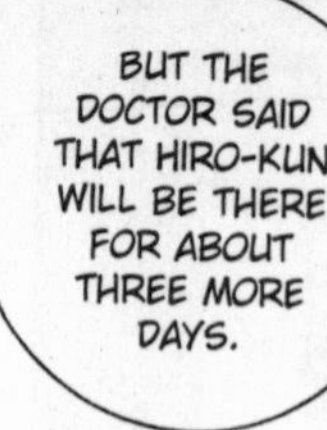
BUT THE DOCTOR SAID THAT HIRO-KUN WILL BE THERE FOR ABOUT THREE MORE DAYS.

I'VE TALKED THINGS OVER WITH MY WIFE HERE, SO HOW ABOUT IT? WHY DON'T YOU COME STAY WITH US UNTIL YOU SETTLE DOWN?
AH...
THANK YOU VERY MUCH.

THAT WAS SUCH AN AWFUL THING THAT HAPPENED TO YOU. I NEVER IMAGINED SOME-THING LIKE THAT COULD EVER HAPPEN...
ANYWAY, I DID PROMISE YOUR PARENTS I'D COUNSEL YOU HALF A YEAR. THOUGH I DON'T THINK YOU'RE IN ANY CONDITION FOR COUNSELING.

IF ANYTHING COMES UP, JUST GIMME A CALL. I THINK I CAN BE OF SOME HELP.
...YES.

YOU'RE PARENTS HAD A LIFE INSURANCE PLAN. IF ANYTHING WERE TO HAPPEN TO THEM, THEY MADE IT SO YOU WOULD RECEIVE A CERTAIN AMOUNT OF MONEY.
THE DETAILS ARE ON THIS PAPER. CAN I GET YOUR SIGNATURE ON THIS FORM HERE...?

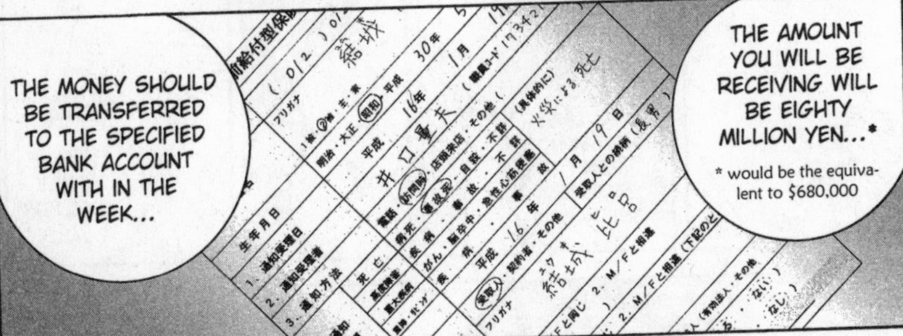
THE AMOUNT YOU WILL BE RECEIVING WILL BE EIGHTY MILLION YEN...*
* would be the equivalent to $680,000
THE MONEY SHOULD BE TRANSFERRED TO THE SPECIFIED BANK ACCOUNT WITH IN THE WEEK...

YOU MEAN YOU DON'T REMEMBER ANYTHING?
SERIOUSLY? I KNOW YOU'VE JUST LOST YOUR PARENTS AND YOU'RE IN BAD SHAPE...

BUT, WHY? WHY DID THAT THING RUN INTO YOUR HOUSE?
DO YOU HAVE SOME KIND OF RELATIONSHIP WITH THAT THING?
...
I DON'T KNOW.

THEN, IF YOU'LL EXCUSE ME.
Swsh
OH, YEAH.
!
THERE ARE REPORTERS EVERYWHERE, SO DON'T TELL THEM ANYTHING.
JUST LIKE HOW YOU DIDN'T TELL US ANYTHING.
...
Swsh

...

HIRO-KUN...
!
RYOKO...
UM... I WAS... I JUST GOT SURPRISED... ABOUT THAT TIME.

BUT... I WILL FORGIVE YOU.
...
...
YOU'VE HEARD THAT WE WILL BE LIVING TOGETHER FOR A WHILE, RIGHT? I'LL BE LOOKING FORWARD TO IT.
DAD SAID THAT HE WILL COME PICK YOU UP IN THREE DAYS. I'LL SEE YOU LATER.
I'LL SEE YOU THEN.
AH... ALL RIGHT.

DAMMIT!

DAMMIT! THAT MONSTER...

I'LL ARREST YOU FOR SURE!

FOR SURE!

WHOOOOOOOH

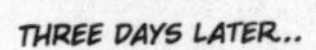

KREEK

AH...

...

WHAT? OH, YOU JUST GOT OUT OF THE BATH...

AH, HIRO-KUN, IT DIDN'T SEEM LIKE YOU ATE EARLIER. ARE YOU ALL RIGHT?
LATER.
YEAH.
Shaw
Thump
GEEZ!
Brrrrr
WHAT'S WITH THAT ATTITUDE?!
RYOKO, HE CAN'T HELP IT. HE LOST HIS PARENTS SO SUDDENLY.
UH-
LET'S LEAVE HIM ALONE FOR A WHILE.
YEAH... I KNOW.
mm
BUT...

NOW FOR THE FOLLOWING NEWS. THE SUSPECT RESPONSIBLE FOR THE CONTINUOUS ASSAULTS IN SETAGAYA AREA HAS BEEN APPREHENDED.
I SEE.

THEY'RE NOT AIRING ANY MORE NEWS ABOUT ME...
THIS IS TANIZAKI AT THE SCENE. AS YOU CAN SEE-

I'M GONNA GO TO BED...
Click

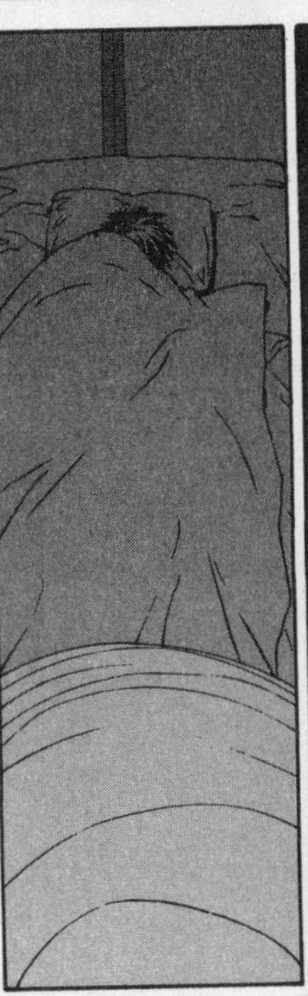

...
THAT WAS...

THAT WAS THE SAME SUIT AS MINE...
Oooo
THE OTHER JUNK...

BUT WHO CAN THAT BE? IT SAID THAT IT LOOKED UP MY INFORMATION. BUT HOW?
WILL I HAVE TO GO SEE IT TO FIND OUT ABOUT IT? DAMMIT! DOES THAT MEAN IT KNOWS MORE ABOUT THE SUIT THAN I DO?
DAMMIT!
Womp
EXCUSE ME.
WHAT'S UP, HIRO-KUN?
RABBLE
ばさっ
THE NEWSPAPERS FROM WHEN I WAS HOSPITALIZED...
WHERE ARE THE ARTICLES ABOUT ME?
THERE.
Snip
ジョキ

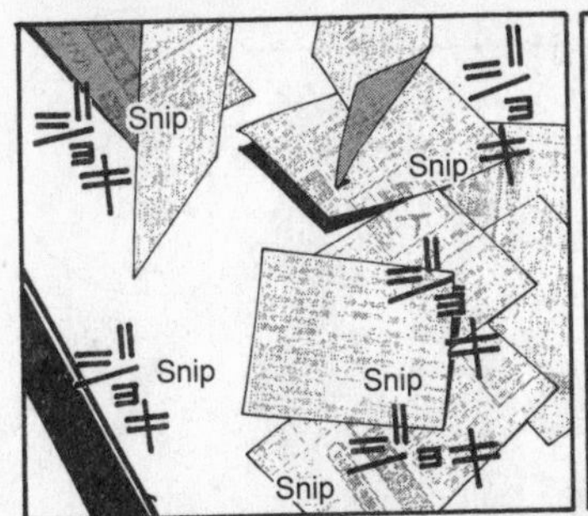

ジョキ Snip
ジョキ Snip
ジョキ Snip
ジョキ Snip

!

ぱく
Hum

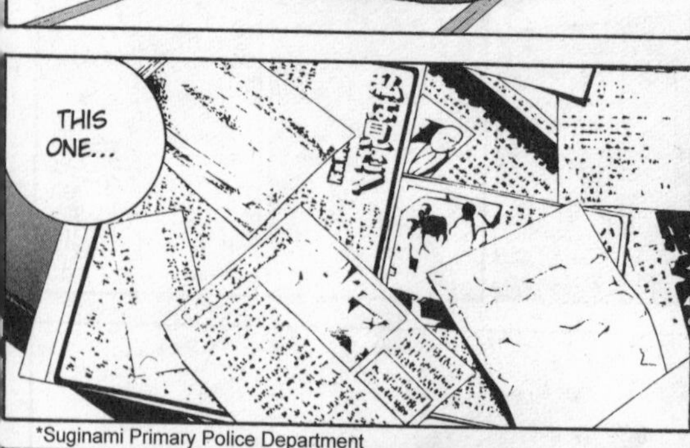

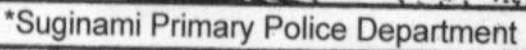
*Suginami Primary Police Department

HMM... SOMETHING BOTHERS ME...

THE ONE WHO SAVED THE DRIVER IN FRONT OF MY EYES, IS THAT THE SAME PERSON WHO ATTACKED MY BROTHER?
DAMMIT. IT WAS AT NIGHT AND IT WAS SO SUDDEN I CAN'T TELL THE DIFFERENCE...

THAT TIME...

IT SEEMS LIKE THEY'RE THE SAME, YET DIF- FERENT AT THE SAME TIME...

AH!
Fwt
IF I REMEMBER CORRECTLY...

THE TV CREW WAS THERE! THE FEMALE REPORTER WAS FROM KTN.
Dash
HEY! FUJIWARA-SAN!

WHERE DID HE TAKE OFF TO THIS TIME?

I'M HOME!

EEK!
HEY.

YOU SCARED ME THERE! WHAT'S UP?
CAN I BORROW YOUR COM-PUTER?

HUH?
IT WILL ONLY TAKE ABOUT A HALF-HOUR..

D... DON'T LOOK AT MY E-MAILS.
I'VE GOT NO INTEREST IN THEM.

O... OK...

RYOKO HAS A PC...
OH, WELL. THIS IS A HYBRID, SO IT SHOULD BE FINE.

HEY, RYOKO. WHAT ARE YOU DOING OUT HERE IN YOUR UNIFORM?

HIRO-KUN WANTED TO USE MY COMPUTER. HE TOLD ME NOT TO LOOK UNTIL HE'S DONE WITH IT...

JEEZ! WHOSE COMPUTER DOES HE THINK IT IS?!

Snap

CAN HIRO-KUN USE A PC?

*CRANE MAIDEN IS A JAPANESE FOLKTALE WHERE A MAN SAVES A CRANE, AND THE CRANE COMES BACK AS A HUMAN TO RETURN HIS FAVOR.

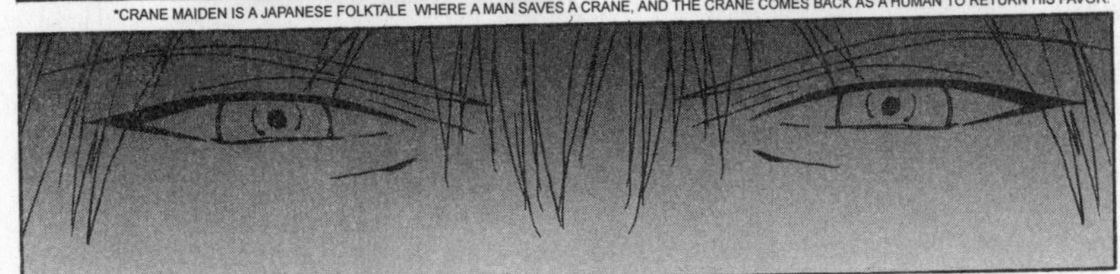

ELCOME TO
JUN
Please connect the USB cable to the computer and follow the directions according to the guidelines.
Version 1.5 Insta
カチ
Click

カチャ
Tap

カチャ
Tap

の登録は完了しま
Version 1.
カチ
Click

ガチャ
KCHNK
OH, ARE YOU DONE?

THANKS.
ス
SS...
...

パタン
SLAM
...

JEEZ.
A CRANE IS MUCH BETTER THAN HE IS!

ヒュウゥゥゥ
WOOOOH

VOICE ENTRY MODE.

カチ

CLICK

CONNECT TO NETWORK.

MAIL SYSTEM, SEND TO: THE OTHER JUNK SYSTEM, TITLE...
ネットに接続しました
It connected with the network.
Junk network systems
JUNK NET EX NO.001

SEND.
Send To: Auto-Search
The Other JUNK System
I'll be waiting.
This is the other JUNK. I want to thank you for what you did for me that day. When you see this e-mail, I want to see you at the following location. Nakano Sun Plaza. I'll be waiting, every day at twelve o'clock.
Converting voice into text.
JUNK NET EX NO.001
LOCATION WILL BE... NAKANO SUN PLAZA PERIOD. NEXT LINE... I'LL BE WAITING, EVERY DAY AT TWELVE O'CLOCK PERIOD.
WOOOO
FWOOOO
POP
送信しました。
Mail was transmitted.
Junk network systems
JUNK NET E

OOOO
WOOOO

NAVIGATION MODE, SEARCH OPTION!

KTN
関東テレビジョン
ネットワーク
KANTO TELEVISION NETWORK

CAN YOU GO ON TO THE NEXT ONE?

Pop

...

STOP!

CAN YOU BRING UP THE EARLIER PICTURE ON ANOTHER MONITOR?

C5

C6

...

THIS IS THE ONE THAT SAVED THE DRIVER...

AND THIS IS THE ONE THAT CRASHED INTO THE HOUSE.

ARE THEY... ONE AND THE SAME? NOW THAT I SEE THEM LIKE THIS...
THEY SEEM LIKE THEY ARE TWO DIFFERENT PEOPLE.

TWO... MYSTERY MEN?
VVVVVVV
...

IT'S BEEN THIRTY MINUTES ALREADY...
DAMMIT... WILL IT NOT APPEAR TONIGHT?
SHOULD'VE BROUGHT MY CHARGER.
YOU CALLED?
!

WHAT'S YOUR
BUSINESS?

ゴオォ
WOOO
(CT-7)
Y... YEAH, I CALLED YOU. I JUST WANTED TO THANK YOU FOR THAT TIME.

THANK...
?
YOU!
Voom
Whack
DO I REALLY HAVE TO TEACH YOU A LITTLE LESSON?
YOU REALLY ARE A KID WHO DOESN'T KNOW ANY MANNERS.
TAP
YOU SHOULDN'T CALL SOMEONE UP AND KICK THEM FOR COMING.

BLAM
VASHOOM
I HAVE SOMETHING I WANT TO ASK YOU! WHY DO YOU KNOW SO MUCH ABOUT THIS SUIT?!
HOW DID YOU FIND OUT ABOUT ME?!
DID YOU READ THE MANUAL?
THE MANUAL?
APPARENTLY NOT.
I GOT YOUR INFORMATION STRAIGHT OFF OF YOUR SYSTEM!
DASH
SO CARELESS OF YOU FOR NOT PUTTING IN A PASSWORD PROTECTION!
YOUR REGISTRY INFORMATION! YOUR ACTIVITY RECORD! IT'S ALL OVER THE PLACE!
KABAM
AGH!

I PUT MY PROTECTION O
AS SOON AS I FOUND OUT ABOUT IT!
VZZT
THAT'S WHY YOU CAN'T ACCESS ANY OF MY INFORMATION!
WHOA!

Kablam
EEEE-
EEK!!
Crackle
BOOM
CRACKE
WHAT IS IT? SOMETHING FELL DOWN!
RATTLE
WOOOOH
A GOD? A DEVIL?
THE LAST TIME WE MET I ASKED YOU A QUESTION! SO, WHICH DID YOU CHOOSE TO BECOME?
!
THAMP

KABOOM
I'VE MADE MY DECISION.
Crackle
I WILL BECOME A GOD!
A GOD!
THUMP

JUSTICE 3: JUNK FIGHT

PEOPLE CALL THOSE GODS DEVILS.
オオオ
OOOOOO

JUSTICE 3: JUNK FIGHT

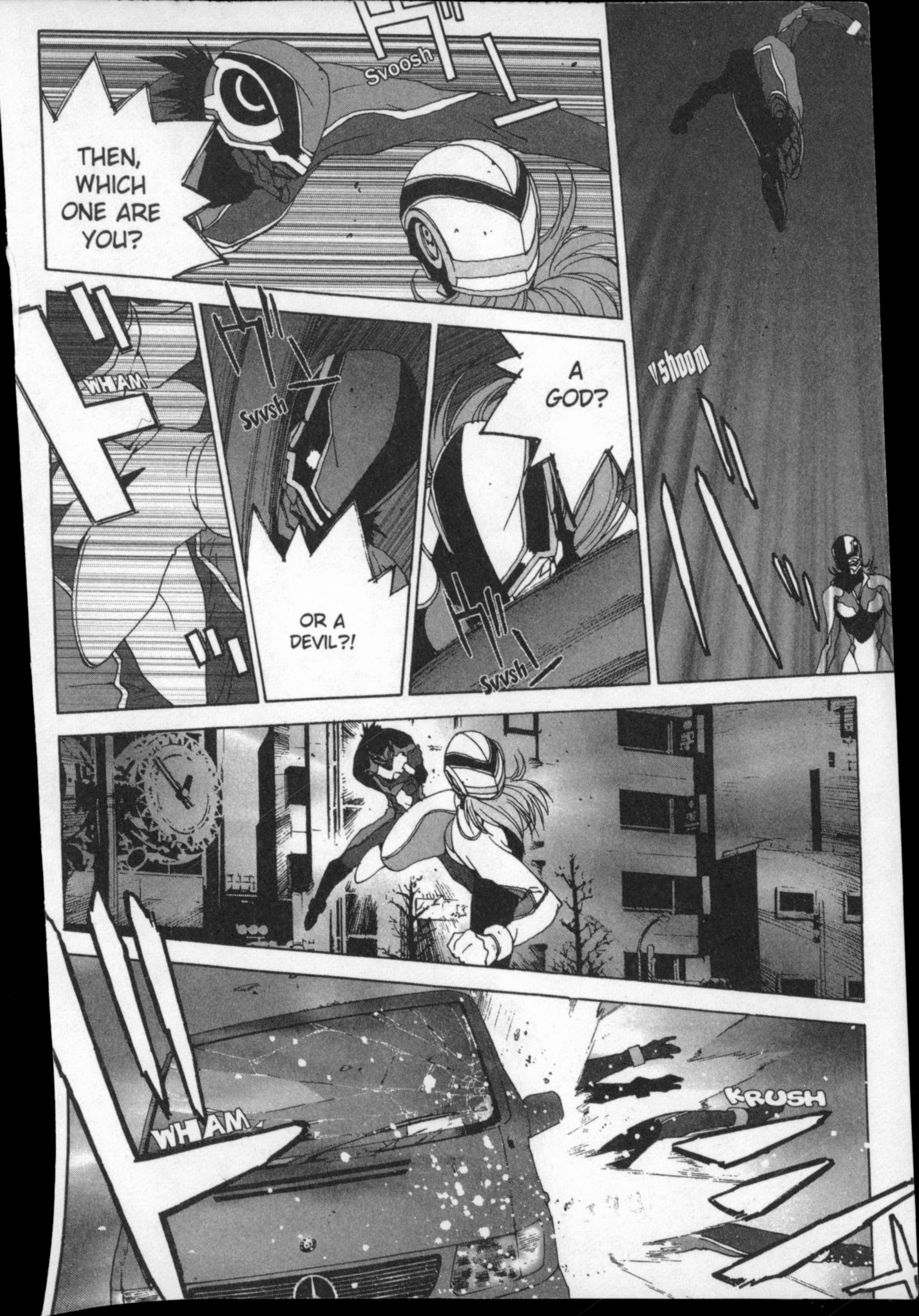

Svoosh

THEN, WHICH ONE ARE YOU?

WHAM

Svvsh

A GOD?

OR A DEVIL?!

Svvsh

Vshoom

WHAM

KRUSH

I SEE...
Crckle
THAT IS UP FOR THE OTHERS TO DECIDE.
Thump
TO TELL YOU THE TRUTH, I'M ACTING ONLY AS I PLEASE, TOO.
AT LEAST WE HAVE SOMETHING IN COMMON.
I WILL ACT ONLY AS I PLEASE.
OUCH...

VROOOM
BEEP
BEEP

CRACK
WHOA!

WE'RE NOT MOVING AT ALL.
EVEN ON NAKANO ST., THERE SHOULDN'T BE THIS MUCH TRAFFIC.

OW...
Crackle

VSHOOM
SHATTER

...
...
Crckle
Kwhack

KaBoom
HEY, ISN'T THAT...

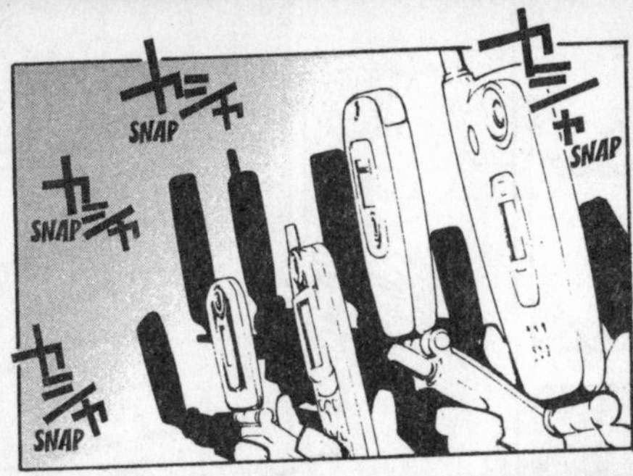
SNAP
SNAP
SNAP
SNAP

INCREDIBLE
...

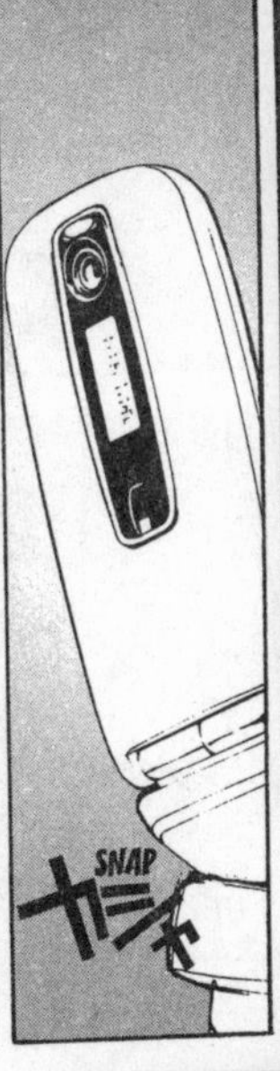
SNAP

SNAP

THIS IS THE POLICE DEPARTMENT, HOW CAN WE HELP YOU?

U... UM... THEY'RE FIGHTING IN FRONT OF NAKANO STATION.
E-EXCUSE ME? FIGHTING?

UM.. THE SUGINAMI MYSTERY MAN WHO WAS ON TV...
P... PLEASE STAY ON THE LINE!

KTN
関東テレビジョン
ネットワーク

YES.

IN NAKANO?

YE...

HEY! FUJIWARA-SAN!

...

HEY! THERE'S A NEWSFLASH. A NEWSFLASH.

VSHOOM

KATHUM

AH!

アッ危ない
そのスピードが
Boom

Ka
交通安全
中野駅
RTTLE
RTTLE
RTTLE

GRRRM

RTTLE
RTTLE
RTTLE
RTTLE

KRASH
ACK...

SHOOT!
BLEEP
05:48:7

I'M RUNNING OUT OF TIME AGAIN...
DAMMIT! GOTTA DO OMETHING.

HURRY.
I HAVE TO HURRY AND GET OUT OF HERE... OR ELSE I'LL HAVE NOWHERE TO RUN...
WOBBLE

I SEE THAT YOU'VE RUN OUT OF TIME.

THUMP

FFFFFF

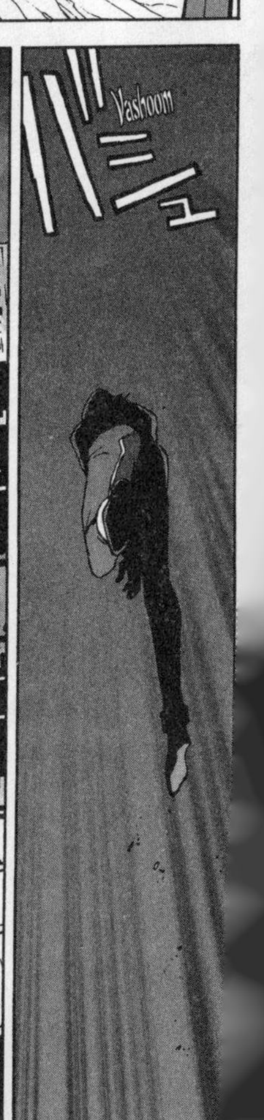
Vashoom

Wooh
Wooh
Wooh
Wooh

Bam

DAMMIT! IT GOT AWAY AGAIN!

KAJI! IT'S ME, FUJIWARA! WHERE ARE YOU RIGHT NOW?
AH, FUJI-WARA-SAN. I'M IN FRONT OF SUN PLAZA RIGHT NOW.

WHAT'S THE SITUATION?!
Wooh
Wooh
Wooh

WOOH
WOOH

ひた
Thap
ひた
Thap
Thap
ひた

TICK, TICK, TICK. WHAT KIND OF A HERO IS LIMITED ON TIME?
AH... ULTRAMAN IS ALSO LIMITED ON TIME.

COMPARED TO THAT, I GUESS AN HOUR IS PRETTY GOOD.

TAX...
OH, YEAH... I FORGOT THAT I DON'T HAVE ANY CASH ON ME.
!

!
キイ
CREEK
PHEW
ガチャ
THUMP

THIS IS FROM THE SCENE...
UH...

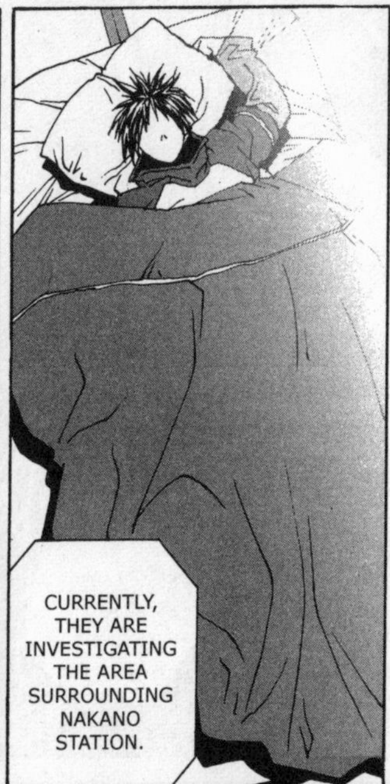
CURRENTLY, THEY ARE INVESTIGATING THE AREA SURROUNDING NAKANO STATION.

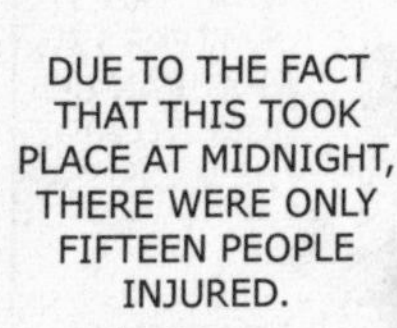
DUE TO THE FACT THAT THIS TOOK PLACE AT MIDNIGHT, THERE WERE ONLY FIFTEEN PEOPLE INJURED.

AF... *YAWN*

THIS PHOTOGRAPH WAS TAKEN BY ONE OF THE WITNESSES... YES, THIS IS THE ONE.
TAKE A LOOK AT THIS PHOTOGRAPH.

CAN YOU SEE? IT SEEMS THAT THERE WERE TWO MYSTERY MEN, AFTER ALL.
BUT... WHAT ARE THEY...?
Dripple
Dripple
Dripple

PHEW
THERE CAN BE MANY POSSIBLE ANSWERS TO THIS, BUT THE THING WE MUST BE MOST CONCERNED WITH RIGHT NOW IS THE FACT THAT THE POLICE HAVE NOT BEEN ABLE TO TAKE ANY PREVENT-ATIVE MEASURES.

WHAT TRULY MATTERS IS WHAT CAN BE DONE TO AID THE VICTIMS.
Midnight Nakano Astonished! Who are the two mystery men?
NAKANO SUN PLAZA AND NAKANO STATION ARE ANOTHER PROBLEM WE HAVE TO FACE.

WHO IS GOING TO BE RESPONSIBLE FOR THE DAMAGE CAUSED TO THESE AREAS AND THOSE WHO WERE AFFECTED BY THE SUSPENSION OF THE CENTRAL LINE?
JEEZ...

NOW I KNOW WHY A HERO HIDES HIS TRUE IDENTITY.
THERE'S NO WAY ONE CAN AFFORD SUCH A HUGE AMOUNT OF MONEY.

KNOCK
KNOCK
HIRO-KUN, ARE YOU AWAKE?
Y... YES.

AREN'T YOU HUNGRY? YOU HAVEN'T EATEN ANYTHING SINCE LAST NIGHT, RIGHT?
DO YOU WANT SOMETHING?

UH... AH... ANYTHING IS FINE...

THEN I'LL PREPARE SOME-THING FOR YOU. WHY DON'T YOU TAKE A BATH WHILE I'M AT IT?

ALL RIGHT...
AND NOW FOR THE FOLLOW-ING NEWS.

SIGH

IT HAS BEEN CONFIRMED THAT THERE ARE TWO MYSTERY MEN.
Suginami Primary Police Department
CONFERENCE ROOM A
IT'S OBVIOUS SINCE IT'S ALL OVER THE TV NETWORK AND THERE ARE MANY WITNESSES.

SO, WHAT EXACTLY ARE THEY?
...

WHAT DO YOU THINK?

IF... EVEN IF THERE IS AN OPPORTUNITY TO CATCH THEM...
...EVEN SO?

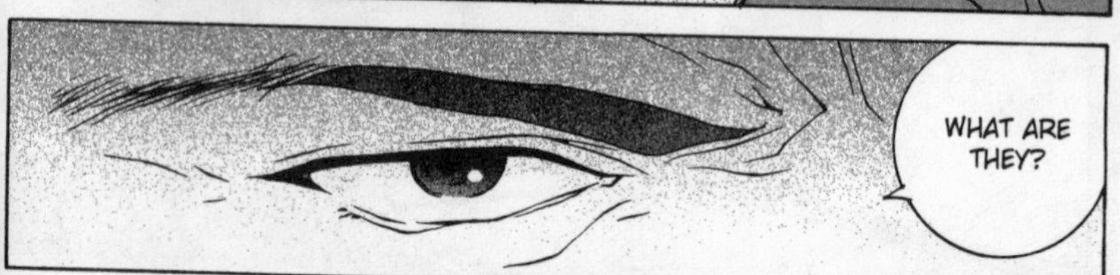
WHAT ARE THEY?

IS IT POSSIBLE FOR US TO ARREST THEM?

...

HOW ABOUT REQUESTING THE AID OF THE SELF-DEFENSE FORCE...

RELYING ON THE SELF-DEFENSE FORCE WHEN POLICE CANNOT HANDLE IT...
YOU WATCH TOO MANY MOVIES.

ガチャ
fwap
DAMMIT. IT HURTS.
THAT ONE... WAS A WOMAN... WASN'T SHE?
EVEN IF SHE HAD READ THE MANUAL, CAN THERE BE THAT MUCH OF A DIFFERENCE IN POWER?
WHAT IS IT WITH THAT SUIT'S POWER?

AH... IT'S FINE.

YOU CAN JUST LEAVE THE LAUNDRY AS IT IS.
I'LL WASH THEM FOR YOU.

THERE. EAT WELL.

IT'S ALL RIGHT; I'M JUST GOING TO WASH THEM ALL TOGETHER.

I SEE...

THE NEXT TOPIC IS ABOUT MS. MANAMI HIRAGI'S LIVE TOUR, *THE* BEST DVD, AND HER FIRST PHOTOGRAPH COLLECTION. IS THAT CORRECT, KUMAKAWA-SAN?
THAT'S CORRECT. THIS APRIL IS THE THIRD ANNIVERSARY OF HER DEBUT, AND TO CELEBRATE SHE'S HOLDING A SPECIAL JAPANESE TOUR WITH VENUES INCLUDING EACH OF THE FOUR LARGEST DOME STADIUMS IN JAPAN.
G-NEWS
SANYO

BUT THE TICKETS FOR THE CONCERT ARE ALREADY SOLD OUT...
Phwp

AS FOR THE PHOTOGRAPH COLLECTION, THERE WILL BE A LIMITED EDITION AVAILABLE THAT COMES WITH THE MAKING OF THE DVD.
IT'S MANAMI.

IT'S BEEN A WHILE SINCE I SAW HER LAST...

OH, YEAH... HER NEW SINGLE IS COMING OUT NEXT WEEK.
BUT MY CONCERT TICKET HAS TURNED INTO ASHES.

WHAT TO DO...
IF I GET A TICKET ON EBAY, IT WILL BE UNDOUBTEDLY EXPENSIVE...

ONE OF THE LOCATIONS WILL BE AT SHOSEN BOOKMART IN KANDA...

I KNOW. ONLY THE FAN-CLUB MEMBERS CAN GO.

MANAMI'S GOING TO APPEAR IN FRONT OF THE FANS FOR THE FIRST TIME, OTHER THAN AT HER TV RECORDINGS AND CONCERTS.

ROLL

SIGH. SERIOUSLY THINGS ARE SO HARD FOR ME NOW.

I CAN'T EVEN GO OUT TO BUY MANAMI'S CD. AND I CAN'T EVEN TRANSFORM AND GO OUT...

I SHOULD... MOVE OUT OF HERE.

Glimpse

HIRO-KUN SHOULD COME BACK TO SCHOOL NOW.

ALL OF THE BULLIES THAT PICKED ON HIM HAVE BEEN HOSPITALIZED...

?

BUT WHY WERE THEY SINGLED OUT AND ATTACKED?

WHY?

IT'S SO BRIGHT...

THE OUTSIDE IS... REALLY WHITE...

Slam

OH...
ISN'T THAT UNUSUAL?

VROOOOOOOOOM

THANK YOU FOR WAITING. THIS WILL BE YOUR NEW BANK BOOK.
Mizuho Bank
AH... THANK YOU.

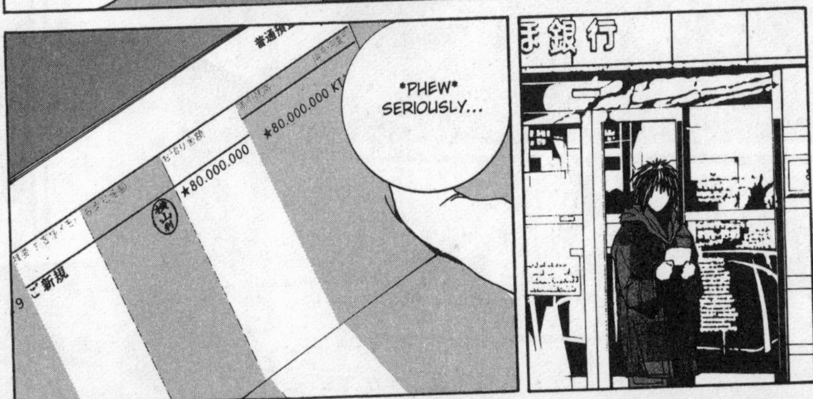
銀行
PHEW SERIOUSLY...
★80.000.000
★80.000.000
ご新規

THIS IS FABULOUS.

004 SPRING——SUMMER LIVE TOUR

HIIRAGI

04 SPRING——SUMMER LIVE TOUR

MANA

YES.

DOES IT SUIT YOUR TASTE?

...

AH...

IF THERE IS ANYTHING I CAN DO,

FEEL FREE TO LET ME KNOW.

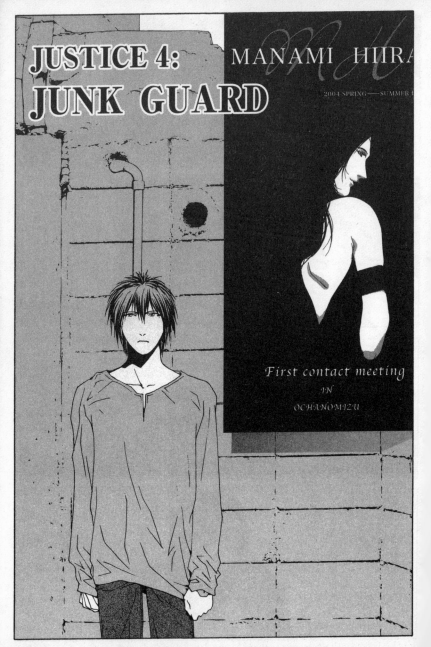

JUSTICE 4: JUNK GUARD

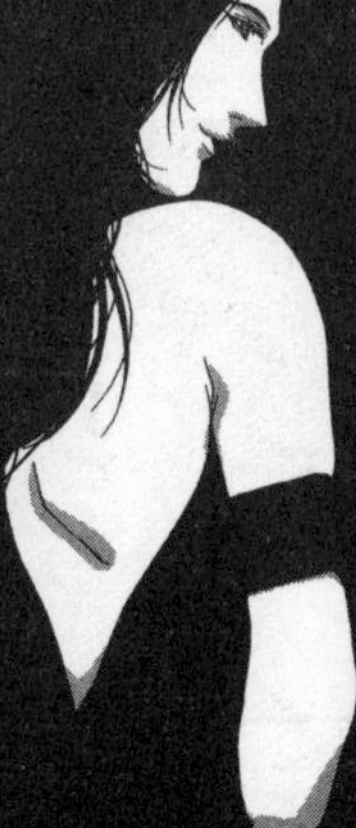

TAKE A LOOK AT THIS. THIS IS THE FOOTAGE FROM THE MORNING AFTER THE INCIDENT.
IT HAS BEEN THREE DAYS SINCE THE INCIDENT, BUT THE JR CENTRAL LINE IS STILL SUSPENDED.

THIS AFFECTS THE MILLIONS OF COM-MUTERS WHO USE THE JR DAILY AS THEIR PRIMARY MODE OF TRANS-PORTATION. JR HAS BEEN BUSY SENDING OUT EXTRA BUSES TO RESOLVE THIS PROBLEM.
...

AS YOU CAN SEE, NAKANO SUN PLAZA IS ALSO A DISASTER.
AS FAR AS WE CAN TELL FROM THE INFORMA-TION THAT HAS BEEN OBTAINED, WE CAN ONLY COME TO ONE CONCLUSION.

THIS DESTRUCTION COULD ONLY BE CAUSED BY A NON-HUMAN BEING.
THIS SURPASSES HUMAN POSSIBILI-TIES. THIS IS NOT LIKE IN THE MOVIES, TV SHOWS, AND MANGA. THIS IS ACTUALLY HAPPENING.

WHY DON'T WE JUST CALL THIS WHITE FEMALE ONE EVE, AND THIS OTHER BLACK MALE ADAM?

HOW ABOUT IT, EVERY-ONE?

CLICK

THEY'RE CALLED JUNK.

KNOCK
KNOCK
MAY I HAVE A WORD WITH YOU, HIRO-KUN?
YES.
...YOU KNOW.
WHAT IS IT?
WHY DON'T YOU COME BACK TO SCHOOL? NOW THAT A NEW TERM HAS BEGUN...
HOW ABOUT IT, HIRO-KUN?!
EVEN IF I GO BACK TO SCHOOL, THEY'RE GOING TO HOLD ME BACK A YEAR.
...
I'LL BE IN A DIFFERENT YEAR FROM YOU, RYOKO.
I... THINK I SHOULD QUIT SCHOOL.
!

HUH...
I'VE BEEN THINKING ABOUT IT FOR A WHILE.
WHY ARE YOU SO SURPRISED?
UMM... UH... HM... YEAH.
I JUST DIDN'T EXPECT THAT.
I SEE.
I SEE...
SO, YOU'RE GOING TO QUIT...
SCHOOL...
YEAH.

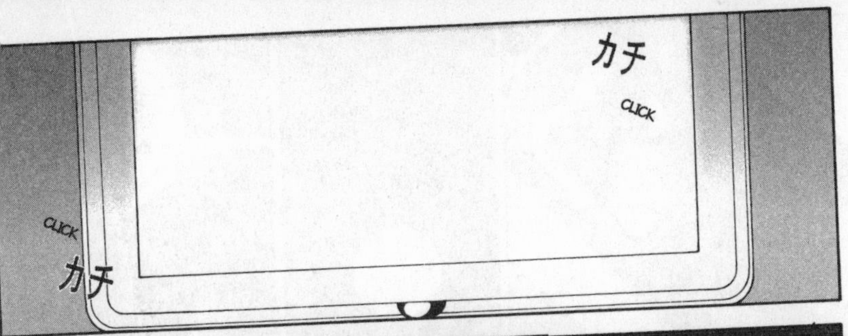

Auction>Ticket>Idol>Female

Manami Hiiragi Autograph Session Ticket! Only Available for Fan Club Members! Buy It Now Available

CLICK
カチ

CLICK カチ

The seller will pay for shipping

Deposit Payment
Electronic Cash

The seller will

Current Bid 88000円

Number of Bids 25件

Preferred Bidding Amount 100000円

Time Left 1Day 1日

カチ CLICK

●Are you sure you want to bid with this amount?

100000円 BID

CLICK カチ

Congratulations! You have won the Bid!

Item you have won: Manami Hiiragi Autograph Session Ticket! Only Available for Fan Club Members! Buy It Now Available

The seller will contact you shortly, so please wait. If the seller does not contact you then—

I CAN PAY 100000 YEN IN NO TIME.

バタ！

Slam

HIRO-CHAN.

!

AUNTIE.

I HEARD THAT YOU ARE PLANNING TO MOVE OUT OF THIS HOUSE. YOU CAN STAY HERE AS LONG AS YOU WANT...

AH...

BUT...

I WILL BE MOVING OUT SOON.

...I SEE.

PLEASE KEEP IN TOUCH.

...YES.

Ooooooh
Ooooooh
Woooo

Flap
Real Estate
WANT TO BUY
WANT TO SELL
Flap

CRACKLE

I KNEW IT ALL ALONG...

THAT IT WOULD COME TO THIS...
売出現地

㈱プロネット

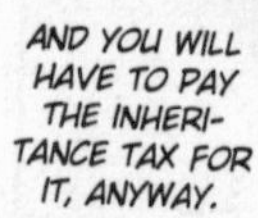
HIRO, ARE YOU LISTENING TO ME? I THINK IT IS BEST FOR YOU TO SELL THAT LAND.
AND YOU WILL HAVE TO PAY THE INHERITANCE TAX FOR IT, ANYWAY.
AH.
THE ONLY THING THAT YOUR PARENTS WERE ABLE TO LEAVE YOU IS THAT LAND,
AH.

I'LL JUST LEAVE IT ALL UP TO YOU.

チャリーン
Clink
...

I SEE.
SO I
HAVE LOST
EVERYTHING...

IS IT ALL RIGHT TO TALK NOW?
I'VE HEARD THAT YOU'VE BEEN GOING OUTSIDE LATELY.
!

TSUJIDO-SAN...
GET IN.
IT'S A NICE DAY TO GO ON A DRIVE.
A... ALL RIGHT.
THAT'S GOOD TO HEAR.
VVROM
SO, I'VE HEARD THAT YOU'RE MOVING OUT OF THAT HOUSE.
IT SEEMS LIKE YOU KNOW EVERYTHING.
RYOKO'S MOTHER TOLD ME. I SUPPORT YOUR DECISION. BESIDES, ONCE YOU START LIVING BY YOURSELF, IT WILL BE EASIER FOR ME TO VISIT YOU.
RRR
RRR
VRRR

...
I SEE THAT COUNSELORS EARN A LOT. ISN'T THIS CAR A PORSCHE?
HA HA HA! YOU THINK SO? JUST BECAUSE I'M IN A PORSCHE, YOU ASSUME I MAKE A LOT OF MONEY? I THINK YOU BASE YOUR OPINIONS TOO MUCH ON APPEARANCES.
UUU
VVUU
THOUGH I'M PRETTY SURE THAT THERE ARE SOME WHO MAKE QUITE A BIT...
I WAS BARELY ABLE TO AFFORD THIS WITH A FIVE-YEAR LOAN.
VOO
PORSCHE
STUTTGART
A GUY WHO GETS A NEW CAR EVERY THREE YEARS...
AND A GUY WHO'S OWNED A PORSCHE FOR OVER TEN YEARS. WHICH SOUNDS BETTER?
UUU
I SEE...
I DON'T KNOW.
UUU
HA HA, I SEE.

THIS PLACE HAS JUST BEEN BUILT, SO YOU CAN LIVE PRETTY COMFORTABLY.

IS YOUR BROTHER GOING TO START LIVING BY HIMSELF?

SOMETHING ... LIKE THAT.

IT'S ONE OF THE DESIGNER MANSIONS THAT ARE IN STYLE RIGHT NOW. AROUND HERE, YOU CAN'T GET A BETTER DEAL THAN THIS...

I SEE...

YOU WILL UNDERSTAND WHAT I'M TRYING TO SAY IN THE NEAR FUTURE. IT'S ALL ABOUT THE EXPERIENCE THAT YOU BUILD UP.
YOU'LL UNDERSTAND THE MEANING OF POSSESSING THINGS, AND WHAT USE YOU WILL HAVE OF THEM.

EVEN IF YOU ARE DEPRESSED...

ANOTHER DAY WILL COME...

TOMORROW IS A BIG DAY.

SHOSEN

曲数日本一
カラオケ
パセラ
Live & Party

DARTS
60名

Vroooom

IT'S MANAMI!
IT'S MANAMI!
WALLA
WALLA
MANAMI!
MANAMI-CHAN.
WALLA
MANAMI!
MANAMI
!!!

WALLA
WALLA
I CAN'T... SEE...

Event Infor
Attention Attendees
Please stand clear of the door
in the passageway.
ay enter the room only
the door is open
SHOSEN
HUH- THEY TOOK HER TO A DIFFERENT ROOM.
WHAT? THEY'RE DOING IT IN THAT ROOM.

PHEW
Thump

WE'RE NOW GOING TO CALL OUT THE NUMBERS ON THE TICKETS. PLEASE HEAD TO THIS SIDE OF THE ROOM.
OF COURSE.
ANAMI
THE PERSON WITH THE TICKET NO.1, PLEASE GO FORWARD.
MANAMI!

I'M...
TICKET NUMBER 25. PLEASE DO WHAT THE STAFF INSTRUCTS YOU TO. THIS TICKET IS VALID ONLY FOR THE DAY. IF LOST, THE TICKET WILL BE VOID.
NUMBER TWENTY-FIVE...

AH... MANAMI-CHAN.

EXCUSE ME. AH... MAY I SHAKE YOUR HAND?

...

UM. AH. SINCE YOUR DEBUT I'VE BEEN...

NEVER MIND THAT. UM, I'VE NEVER SEEN YOU WEAR THAT BEFORE, BUT I THINK...

WILL THE NEXT PERSON WITH NUMBER TWENTY FIVE COME IN?
creek
YE...

RAGI MANAMI
RAGI MAN
ER LIVE TOUR
2004
TOUR
MA...
First con
OCH

MANAMI
2004
SHOSEN
BOOK MART
MANAMI
MANAMI...

...IT'S REALLY HER.
HELLO!

AH...

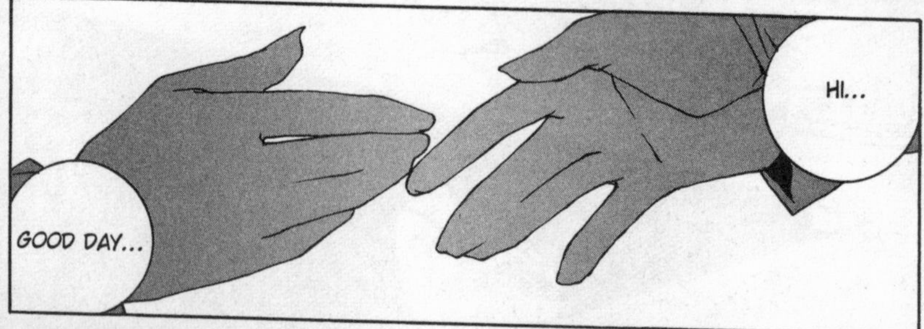
HI...
GOOD DAY...

I-IT'S AN EMERGENCY.
THUMP
THUMP
!
HUH?

SHOSEN
BOOK MART
EXCUSE ME, BUT THERE HAS BEEN A LITTLE PROBLEM SO WE'RE CANCELING THE EVENT NOW.
WHAT? WHAT IS IT, MANAGER?

NAMI
WAIT A SECOND. WHY?
THERE'S A PROBLEM OUTSIDE! THE AUTOGRAPH SESSION HAS BEEN CAN-CELLED.

HUH?
CANCELLED ...

Wait...
OUTSIDE?
IT'S DAN-GEROUS SO HURRY AND GET MANAMI OUT OF HERE.
WHAT'S GOING ON?

MANAMI!
KNK

IF THE PROBLEM IS SOLVED, WILL YOU GUYS CONTINUE ON WITH THE AUTO-GRAPH SESSION?

WE DON'T KNOW.

DAMMIT ...

Thump

Thump

Thump

THERE'S SOME WEIRDO RUNNING AMOK OUTSIDE.

WHAT, WHY DOES IT HAVE TO BE NOW?

Thump

THEY'LL CONTINUE ON WITH MANAMI'S AUTOGRAPH SESSION!
ONCE AGAIN!
CAUSING TROUBLE AT SUCH AN IMPORTANT TIME!
I WON'T FORGIVE YOU!

AUGH
!!!
Road blocked due to pedestrians
Restricting traffic from 11a.m. to 2p.m.
Kanda Police Department Kanda Suzuran Way

BRING HER TO ME! MY WIFE!
Victoria
GEAR

IS IT THAT GUY WITH THE KITCHEN KNIFE?
SO STUPID.
BUT...
IT'S THAT WOMAN AGAIN...
DON'T COME NEAR ME!
THE WHITE JUNK...
QUICK! BEFORE MANAMI LEAVES THIS AREA!
VOSH
I'LL KILL YOU IN A FLASH. YOU KITCHEN-KNIFE BASTARD.
ウクレレ
バイオリン

JUSTICE 5: JUNK JUNCTION

WHAT THE HELL ARE YOU?! DON'T COME ANY CLOSER, YOU BASTARD!
新大久保本店 /
お茶の水1号館
JEEZ, GETTING INVOLVED WITH MORE TROUBLE HERE... *SIGH*
I SHOULDN'T HAVE COME TO KANDA.
IF YOU COME ANY CLOSER... HA HA.
I'M NOT AFRAID TO DIE!
UH HEH HEH.
Slip
SIGH
ANALYZING THE SITUATION, THERE IS A HIGH CHANCE THAT... HE'S A DRUG ADDICT...
AN AMPHET-AMINE OF SOME KIND...

WAIT...
IT DOESN'T SEEM LIKE I'LL HAVE TO WASTE MY TIME ON THIS GUY...
HMM?
THAT'S...
THAT'S MANAMI!
SERIOUSLY! MANAMI'S LEAVING?!
DAMMIT!
VRRRR

TAKE CARE OF THAT AFTER MANAMI. THAT OVER THERE.

THUM

THUM

THUM

THUM

ALL RIGHT! ALL RIGHT! WE'RE GETTING ON IT RIGHT

CAMERA, OVER HERE. OVER HERE!

IS THE REPORT READY YET? HEY! HURRY WITH IT!

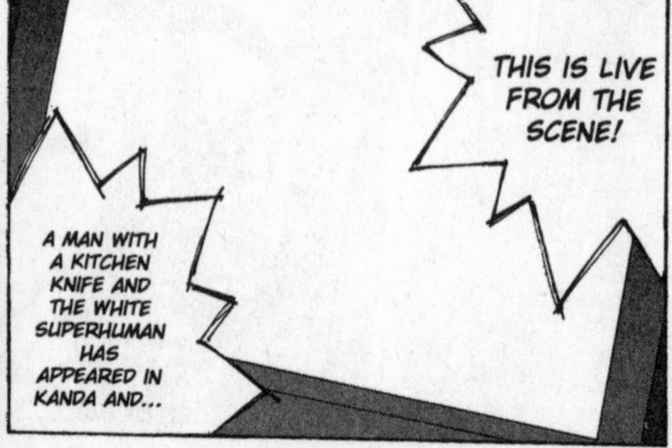

SVSH
SVSH
K
AIEEE-YAH!
HE... WHAT ARE YOU??

GRM

THUNK

WHA...

ガラー

CLINGG

SCREEK
SCREEK
SCREEK
CASHIER
Crun
Crun
KKKK
WHA... WHAT'S GOING ON?
!
Ping

書店ビル
自転車通行可
RRUMMM

小川町
KRR

Krack

Thkrm

KRKRKRKRKR

KTHUD
KTHUD

4F
3F
旅行·地図
ノベルス
ファンタジー系文庫

THAT...

BASTARD...

MANAMI ALREADY TOOK OFF!

ダッ
Thump

DAMMIT! WHY ISN'T IT MOVING?! THIS IS A POLICE VEHICLE!
WOOH
WOOH
WOOH
IT CAN'T BE HELPED. WE'RE TRYING TO GET TO THE CAUSE OF THE TRAFFIC.

WE'RE GONNA RUN!
Kcreek
WHAT? RUNNING TO KANADA? FROM THE YASUKUNI SHRINE?

WHEN YOU RETURN TO THE STATION, TELL THE POLICE AFFAIRS DEPART-MENT TO SUPPLY FOLDABLE BICYCLES IN THE

THAT'S ABSURD! CHIEF WILL GET PISSED AT ME!
THU
THU
THU

I CAN'T DEAL WITH THIS.

WELL, IT IS FASTER TO RUN.
HHONK

WHO WOULD DO SUCH A THING...?

NO... THE ONLY PERSON CAPABLE OF SUCH THING IS...

YOU'RE CORRECT!

!

WOOOO

I GOT PISSED BECAUSE OF THAT GUY!

WHAT?

NO... NEVER MIND THAT. ANYWAY, HE GOT IN MY WAY!

YOU...

ズ
ズ
ズ
SOMETHING WRONG WITH THAT?

JUST LIKE HOW YOU KILLED YOUR PARENTS.

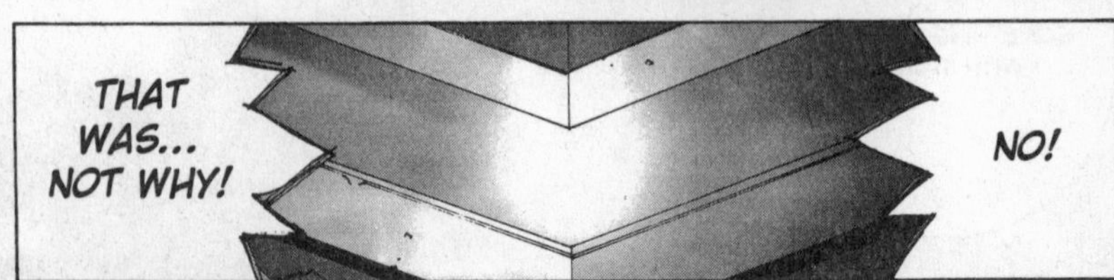

I'M NOT... LIKE THAT!
Wosh
IT WAS AN ACCIDENT... NO, I'M NOT SURE WHAT IT WAS.
ISN'T THAT HOW... IT ENDED UP?
I DON'T KNOW!
DON'T...
ACCUSE ME!
VSH
KRNK
STOP IT!

IF WE FIGHT, YOU SHOULD KNOW THE CONSE-QUENCE...
YOU WANT TO MAKE THIS PLACE BECOME LIKE NAKANO?
KBLAM
YOU'RE MAKING ME DO THIS.
EEEK!
Swooosh
WA... WAAA...
JUNK SYSTEMS SURE DID SEND ONE HELL OF A TOY TO YOU!
EVERYTHING'S ABOUT YOU!
IT GETS ON MY NERVES!

LISTEN UP, YOU COM-MONERS! I'M GOING TO MAKE ONE HELL OF A MESS HERE!

IF YOU DON'T WANT TO DIE, GET THE HELL OUTTA HERE!

THE... THE MYSTERY MAN SPOKE...

THE MYSTERY MAN...

SPOKE...

WHAT ARE YOU SAYING?

KRASH

!!

WHY IS IT THAT THERE ARE TWO OF THESE SUITS?!
ONLY ONE HERO!
CRK
CRK
CRK
THERE SHOULD BE ONLY ONE!

IDIOT!

HE TRULY IS AN IDIOTIC CHILD.

WAAAAAAH
THUD
THUD
EEEEEEEK
THUD
THUD

KRASH
SWOOOM
KABOOM
SOMEONE, HELP ME!
wOOOO
OOOO
EEEEEK!
CAMERA! GET THE CAMERA!
?
WHERE IS SHE? I CAN'T SEE... OH, YEAH, THERE'S THE SEARCH MODE.

VZZOOM
HEY, KID! DID YOU READ THE MANUAL?
ACK!
VASHOOM
KaBoom
!!
?!
ERROR? FOR WHAT?
WARNING
SYSTEM ERROR
Oxygen supply
Beep
OXY... GE...N?
OXYGEN?
Beep
Beep
I DID READ IT...
Thud
GCK...
CRMBLE

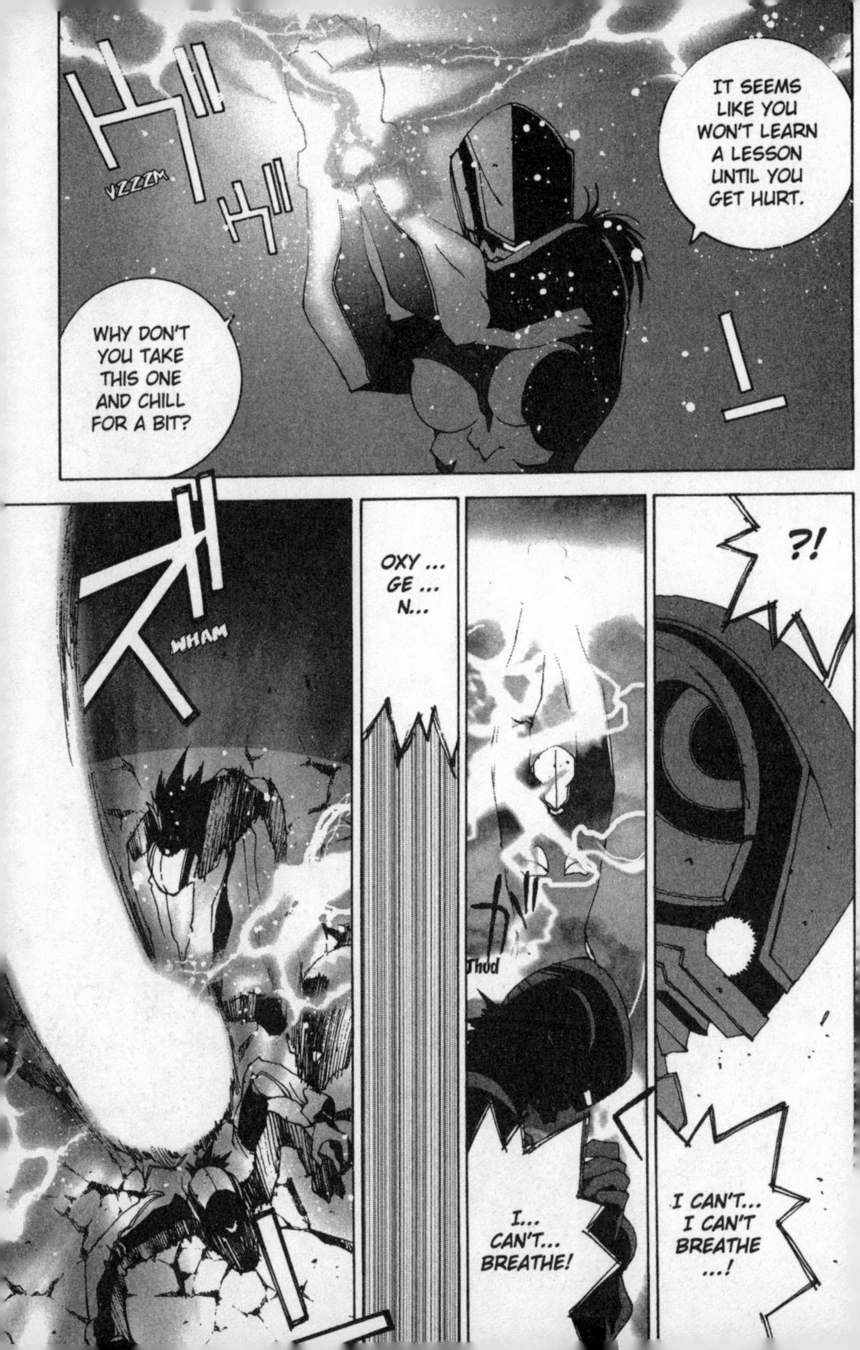

VZZZM

IT SEEMS LIKE YOU WON'T LEARN A LESSON UNTIL YOU GET HURT.

WHY DON'T YOU TAKE THIS ONE AND CHILL FOR A BIT?

?!

I CAN'T... I CAN'T BREATHE ...!

OXY ... GE ... N...

Thud

I... CAN'T... BREATHE!

WHAM

ノーボード用品
徹底値下げ
SPORTS
ペン神田店
OOOM
Dr. Sound

KLABOO
crrack
コンサイス
WOOOOAAA

kbam

Wwoosh
WOW!

...
CRUMBLE
CRUMBLE

DCK
CRUMBLE

DCK
DCK
DCK

THE STRETCHER! OVER HERE!
IT'S DANGEROUS! GET BACK!
PRESERVE THE SCENE! GET IN POSITION!

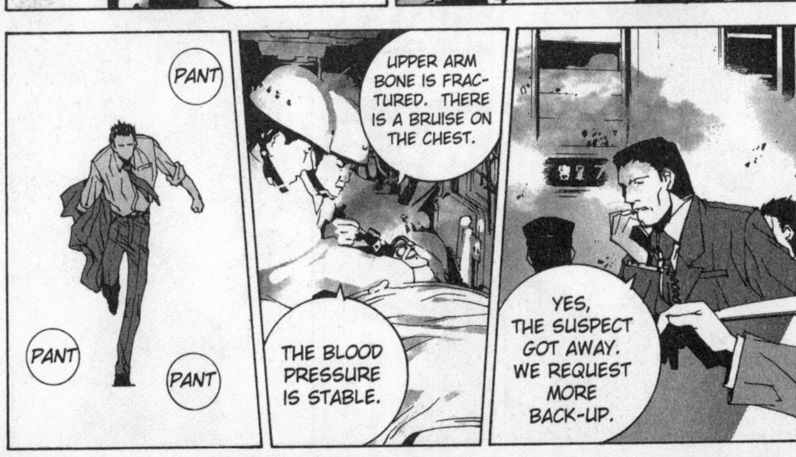
YES, THE SUSPECT GOT AWAY. WE REQUEST MORE BACK-UP.
UPPER ARM BONE IS FRACTURED. THERE IS A BRUISE ON THE CHEST.
THE BLOOD PRESSURE IS STABLE.
PANT
PANT
PANT

TH... THIS IS AWFUL.

Wooh
Wooh

SKRRRRRP
KEEP OUT 立入

WHAT SHOULD WE DO, FUJI-WARA-SAN?
WE'LL, WE CAN'T DO ANYTHING HERE SINCE IT'S THE MOBILE INVESTIGATION TEAM'S JOB.

YES, IT SEEMS LIKE THERE IS NOTHING FOR US TO DO HERE.
LET'S GO BACK.

IT SEEMS LIKE THEY RAN AWAY, AS WELL.

KEEP OUT 立入禁止

HEH... HEH HEH.
GOT NEW INFO!

Wooh
Wooh

Wooh
Wooh
Wooh
Wooh
Wooh

DON'T GET ME WRONG. I'M ONLY DOING THIS BECAUSE WHEN YOU GET CAUGHT BY THE POLICE,
I'LL BE IN TROUBLE, TOO.

THE MANUAL ALSO SAID THAT YOU MUST KEEP THIS A SECRET UNDER ANY CONDITION.
FWSH
DEACTIVATE.

SIGH. IS THERE ANY WAY TO CHANGE THIS DEACTIVATION KEY...?

I DON'T REALLY LIKE THE WORD DEACTIVATE. I WISH I COULD CUSTOMIZE IT TO ANY WORD I LIKE.

WOOH
WOOH
WOOH
8 - 20
りそな銀行

Nakano,
Suginami,
Kanada
Multiple
Destruction
Case Special
Investigation
H.Q.

SO, THEY CAME TO OUR DEPARTMENT. IT TOOK LONGER THAN I THOUGHT IT WOULD, THOUGH.
IT'S PROBABLY BECAUSE THE BLACK AND WHITE FIRST APPEARED OUT OF OUR JURIS-DICTION.

NOW I CAN OFFICIALLY INVESTIGATE.
LOCAL OFFICERS WILL BE LEFT WITH SHITTY TASKS.
WE'VE BEEN LEFT OUT IN THE COLD NOW.

I THINK THIS WILL DO IT.

FUJIWARA-SAN?

...

HEY, THE GUYS FROM THE MAIN OFFICE ARE HERE.
ALL RIGHT!

YOU'D BETTER GET THE TEA PREPARED.
THAT'S A REALLY SHITTY JOB.

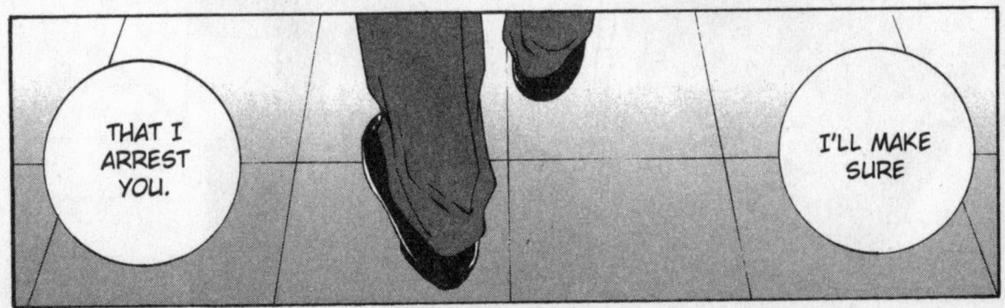
I'LL MAKE SURE
THAT I ARREST YOU.

A SYSTEM ERROR?
ON AN OXYGEN SYSTEM!! I WAS ABOUT TO DIE THERE!

DAMMIT! DAMMIT!
DAMMIT!

CRASH

THAT'S WHY I LOST AGAINST HER!

I'M GOING TO MAKE A CLAIM AGAINST THIS! WHAT IF I DIED BACK THERE?!
DAMMIT!
DAMMIT!

WHAT HAPPENED? WHY ARE YOU SO...?

THIS IS NONE OF YOUR BUSINESS...

...
HMPH...
HMM? HUH.
HA HA HA HA!
SYSTEM
VER. 2
SYSTEM VER. 2

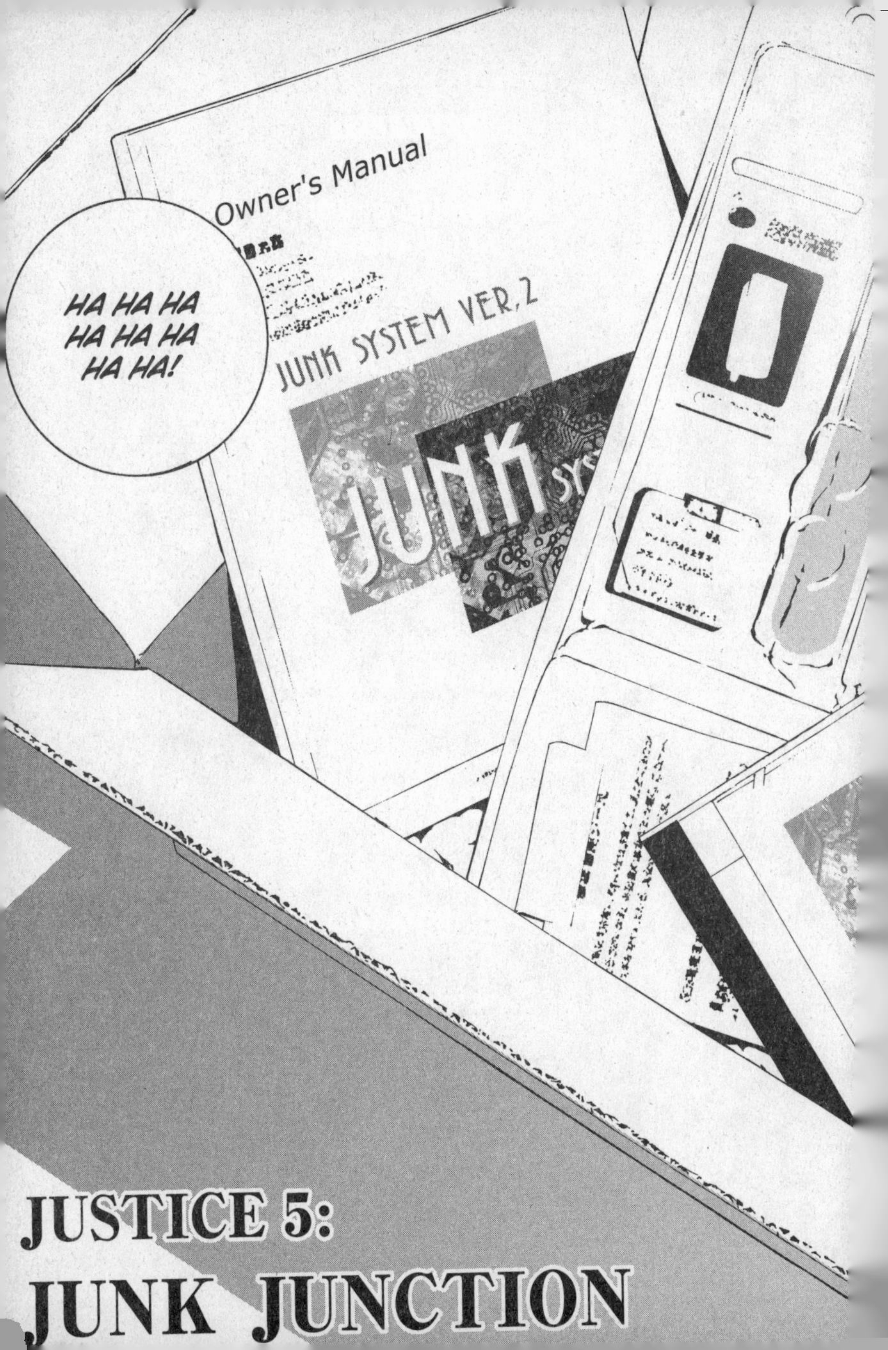

Owner's Manual
JUNK SYSTEM VER.2
JUNK
HA HA HA HA HA HA HA HA!
JUSTICE 5: JUNK JUNCTION

STAFF LIST

art and directed by
KIA ASAMIYA

junk suit design by
YUTAKA IZUBUCHI

art assistant
NAOKI HYODOH
NOBUAKI TAKANO
JUN KANEKO

editor
SHINGO TAKEKAWA(AKITASHOTEN)+α

book designed by
NORIKO IWASHITA

produced by
TAKAFUMI SAWA(AKITASHOTEN)

special thanks to
SUNPLAZA
SHOSEN BOOKMART
ALPINE
and ALL READERS

WHAT'S THIS?

DID YOU KILL THEM?

WOOOOO

ITH YOUR OWN HANDS?

OOOOOO

AAAH!

IT'S NOT A FIGURE?

T IS ..?

WAAA

MANA

MANAMI!

AAAAH

CLICK

SPARE ME SOME ALLOWANCE, WILL YA?

HEY, MISTER.

HIRO-

THERE'S A PACKAGE FOR YOU.

39-06-13

J U N K

RECORD OF THE LAST HERO

PLAY BACK

STOP IT! PLEASE, STOP!
NOOOOO!
WOOOOH
CLICK
CLICK
CLICK
CLICK
HEY...
YOU SHOULD TALK TO HIM, TOO...
Fshhhhh
'VE TOLD HIM ERYTHING I CAN, UT HE REACTS ENTLY SO I CAN'T O ANYTHING.
WHEN WILL HIRO RETURN TO SCHOOL?
THEN, I'LL LEAVE THE COPY OF YESTERDAY'S CLASS NOTES HERE.
...
EZ...

PLAY BACK

If you could choose, which would you decide to become?

A God...

Or... a Devil?

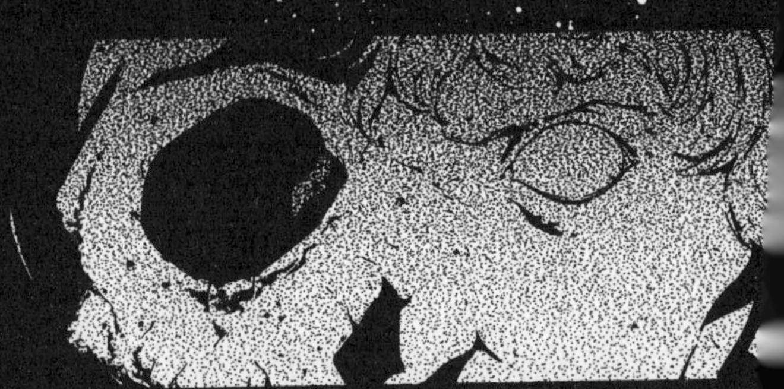